D1168593

a slob in the kitchen

a slob in the kitchen

recipes and entertaining advice from a housewife superstar

karen duffy

Clarkson Potter/Publishers
New York

Published by Clarkson Potter/Publishers, New York, New York
Member of the Crown Publishing Group, a division of Random House, Inc.
www.crownpublishing.com

Printed in the United States of America

Design by Maggie Hinders

Library of Congress Cataloging-in-Publication
Duffy, Karen, 1961–
A slob in the kitchen / Karen Duffy.—1st ed. : recipes and entertaining advice from a housewife superstar
Includes index.
1. Quick and easy cookery. I. Title.
TX833.5.D83 2004
641.5'55—dc22 2003023284

ISBN 1-4000-5115-0

10 9 8 7 6 5 4 3 2 1

First Edition

To Breena Whitcomb, with immeasurable admiration and gratitude.

To John Augustine Lambros, for giving me a deadline.

acknowledgments

I OWE an enormous debt of gratitude to the fabulous home cooks and professional chefs who shared their knowledge with me. Thank you for your guidance and generosity, especially Carol Duffy, Kate Firriollo, Buff DeStephano, Beverly Morris, Sherma Tamby, Jenny Sullivan, and Megan Wilson. It was my great fortune and privilege to work with Pam Krauss, my editor, and her team at Clarkson Potter, with special thanks to Marysarah Quinn. Your faith in and dedication to this project is an honor. David Vigliano and Peg Donegan saw the need for this book and encouraged me as the manuscript developed. Lynn Fischer's wit, creativity, and vision whipped it into shape.

The heftiest recognition must go to Karim Chehimi, who gained nineteen pounds while working with me as research director, recipe taster, joke listener, baby tickler, and career adviser. Your kindness and commitment are an inspiration; thank you.

I dedicate this book, with respect and admiration, to all my fellow Slobs in the Kitchen.

contents

introduction

THIS COOKBOOK is for the host who isn't afraid to crack a few eggs, crack a few jokes, throw a few curves, cut a few corners, and have a few laughs. The expedience of life has made a smoking wreckage of our domestic skills, and in many small ways the fun has been leaking out of our lives. I cook not for some spiritual satisfaction that results from my activities in the kitchen; I cook because my family is hungry, and they get cranky when they don't eat. And when friends drop by, they always seem to expect me to feed them too. Rather than have them stop coming, I've learned a few dishes I can reliably turn out on short notice to an enthusiastic reception.

There are countless thick, hernia-inducing cookbooks with rewardingly honest recipes. This book is not one of them. This book is for people who have better things to do than cook. This book is for scrappy cheats—like me. The recipes in this book are for people who love to eat and drink and entertain but prefer to spend most of their time with family and friends, not in a lonely, dirty, stinking-hot kitchen. Recipes that require your constant vigilance in the kitchen are not included. Proudly included is a recipe for gravy-scented candles, which will make your home smell as if you have been cooking even when you have not.

Don't confuse excellence with complexity.

—ALAN KOEHLER, THE MADISON AVENUE COOK BOOK, 1962

There are rare days when I enjoy making a great effort to prepare a meal. Most days I just want to enjoy a great meal effortlessly. This book is a result of culinary cross-purposes. Perhaps my bisected domestic personality can clarify. My mother is a domestic deity who served her large family a formal dinner six nights a week. With her unimpeachable good taste, she taught me that a good cook cleans as she cooks, and that if you enter and exit the kitchen on a positive note, you create an environment in which you can do your best work. My maternal grandmother, on the other hand, gladly relinquished her birthday cake–baking responsibilities to the Sara Lee Corporation, and served her grandchildren Jiffy Pop and Devil Dogs for dinner. She taught me to smooth the bedcovers right over the heating pad, pill bottles, and cookie boxes. In her book, stirring Sweet'n Low into Sanka was considered cooking. Her attitude toward domestic duty was "Don't be so pious; you'll just have to do it all over again tomorrow, and believe me, there are much more exciting ways to shorten your life!" I am an example of the generation-skipping gene, a culinary split personality. Although raised by a snob in the kitchen, I am a slob in the kitchen. My style is clamorous rather than glamorous.

I did toy with the idea of doing a cookbook. I think a lot of people who hate literature but love fried eggs would buy it if the price was right.

—GROUCHO MARX

I have noticed a dearth of cookbooks that lack pretension. This book is not for the persnickety fusspots who would happily cross state lines in search of heirloom purple tomatoes. Does the world need another cookbook written for the absurdly smug gastronomist? I think that pond has been fished dry. Does the world need a cookbook written by and for scrappy slobs? Well, does Dolly Parton sleep on her back?

Although this book wasn't written for master chefs, or for cooks who exhibit an insane ferocity toward domestic achievement, absolutely every recipe in this wisecracking volume results in a dish that tastes exactly like food. I am confident that this book will teach you some great recipes, as well as a few of the tips and tricks I have up my oven mitt. For example, I advocate hosting two dinner parties on successive nights. Throwing dinner parties a week apart is like getting your breasts surgically enhanced one at a time. You go through all the pain, anxiety, preparation, and expense twice. Since you have already cleaned the house, stocked the bar, arranged the flowers, and cleared the good drugs out of the medicine cabinet, why not double the entrée recipe, bake two desserts, and serve them on back-to-back nights?

The biggest obstacle to cooking and entertaining is not lack of skill; it is lack of nerve. Let me be the Annie Sullivan to your Helen Keller in the kitchen. My mission is to launch you as a practical, imaginative, bold, and subversive cook. I also have to demystify cooking, because it is really quite simple. All food that isn't eaten raw is either boiled, fried, or roasted. Baking, braising, deep-frying, poaching, sautéing, and stewing are just variations of these three basic cooking processes. The majority of the recipes in this book will be done in less time than it would take to order in a pizza. I encourage you to take the shortcut, rather than the scenic route. The kitchen is the most dangerous room in the house, and I want to get you in and out with minimum stress and maximum effect.

I have included many confidence-boosting recipes to help you sharpen your skills. These are indicated with a monkey wearing a dunce cap. But even the more challenging ones can easily be prepared by anyone who can use a measuring cup, a blender, and a cast-iron skillet. All the recipes are breathtakingly simple and delicious—so easy to prepare, in fact, that you will think you are cheating. Well, you are! Before you know it, you will be a regular housewife superstar.

I have invented, experimented, substituted, tested, and rejiggered the recipes and tips in order to make this book deliberately—even ridiculously—easy. All the tricky, bland, and laborious stuff has been sifted out. This may be the only cookbook you'll ever need if you have more adventurous things to do than loiter in your kitchen all day. It is a cheat sheet for fundamental culinary self-esteem and good-natured housekeeping. It is not a road map to mastering the gastronomic arts, but then, you are not the Queen of England, are you?

Cookbooks outsell sex books three to one.

—L. M. BOYD

how to use this book

WHETHER YOU COOK a lot or a little or not at all, this book is going to be your new best friend in the kitchen. Remember, cooking is more than just feeding people. All the recipes are coded to indicate their degree of difficulty. If you're a rank beginner, start with those featuring the monkey in a dunce cap first. Take a crack at a tricky one on an off night of solitude. You can serve it the next night for dinner if the outcome is a success. Practice, so that when you have to perform for an audience you will be confident and self-assured. Impress your guests with your talent; impress them with your courage.

Very easy recipe with few ingredients; will boost your culinary confidence in a snap. Most of the recipes in this book fall into this category.

Graduate to these once you have mastered a few basics. They're slightly more involved than the dunce cap variety but still a cinch to pull off.

When you are feeling frisky in the kitchen try one of these and improve your gastronomic reputation.

time estimates

MOST RECIPES in this volume are designed to get you in and out of the kitchen in less than an hour. So pull yourself up by your bra straps (or jockstrap as the case may be) and make a meal without resorting to the premixed purgatory of cream of mushroom soup.

Of course, the proficiency with which you navigate your way around your scullery will impact the time you spend there. Just know that I won't try to boss you around your own kitchen barking orders. I hope to be more like a friend, with my arm around your shoulder, whispering in your ear, "Come on, you can do it; you're going to be great." And we won't be there all day, I promise.

yields

MOST RECIPES make about four servings, or will feed two people twice. If you are entertaining four to six adults, double the recipe. My goal isn't to have a bunch of leftovers following you around all week, but most dishes improve after their flavors have had a chance to get acquainted during a day in the refrigerator. When in doubt, double it. Nobody likes a stingy host.

Some cookbooks are to be tasted, others to be swallowed, some few to be chewed and digested.

—SIR FRANCIS BACON

A hangover is the wrath of grapes.

—ANONYMOUS

party mix

hors d'oeuvres,

snacks, first courses,

and drinks

without the frenzy

The half hour before dinner has always been considered as the great ordeal through which the mistress, in giving a dinner party, will either pass with flying colors, or lose many of her laurels.

—ISABELLA BEETON,
MRS. BEETON'S BOOK OF HOUSEHOLD MANAGEMENT, 1861

W**HEN THE SUN** goes down, it's party time, and the party starts to swing. **Don't you want to be there, in the thick of it, swinging with your guests?** Who wants to slave in the lonely exile of the scullery, with nothing but some withered olives squinting at you? **Find a recipe you like to eat and don't mind making, and serve it often.** Your old standby soon will be exalted as your specialty. Best of all, you will be relaxed and confident because you know what to expect when you pull it out of the oven.

And if dinner turns out to be less than you expected, don't apologize or make a big deal of it; you will just seem pathetic. Instead, apply the "Rule of Distraction." Encourage your guests to discover their "X-rated name"—derived by combining their first pet's name with their grandmother's maiden name. Most likely, when they recall dinner at your house, they will remember that you are a generous host and that their porn-star name is Bandit Maguire, not that the chicken was overcooked.

The hors d'oeuvre, snack, and first-course **recipes in this section are tasty, fast, and easy, just like your guests.** And I've provided a few general tips below and throughout the chapter to help you simplify your hostess duties.

Most important, loosen up, relax, and have fun. The host sets the tone; if you are uptight or have your knickers in a twist, it will cast a pall on the proceedings. Even if the kitchen is a crazy mess and you are still wearing your yoga pants when the bell rings, greet your guests warmly. If you're not ready, too bad; it's your fault, not theirs. Suck it up and greet every guest and make him or her feel that you're happy to see them and they're welcome to your home.

Elsa Maxwell, a famed hostess of the 1940s and '50s, urged her readers to "serve dinner backwards, do anything—but **for goodness sake, do something weird."**

entertaining shortcuts

Sharing a meal is the foundation of social intercourse. A host needs a sense of buoyancy and immunity from getting weighed down with anxiety. Here is a list of tricks for sidestepping the heavy lifting that comes along with entertaining people.

- **The Wine and Cheese Party:** Set out cheese and fruit platters and pour white and red wine. This is the old-style standby for weaseling out of dinner.
- **The Cocktail Party**: Pass hot hors d'oeuvres and offer a full bar setup.
- **The Tea Party:** Offer sandwiches, scones with cream and jam, tea, and champagne, with fancy cakes you've purchased.
- **Dessert and Coffee:** Serve it at your home after an outing.
- **Brunch:** Set out bagels, smoked salmon, fruit, coffee, pastries, Mimosas and Bloody Marys, crumb buns, and doughnuts. Practically everything is brought in the night before if you're a smart cookie.
- **The Picnic:** Meet friends at an outdoor location; you provide the food and drink and a sexy blanket to stretch out on.
- **The Potluck**: Everyone pitches in.
- **The Progressive Dinner:** Organize a different course at each neighbor's home and enjoy cocktails and hors d'oeuvres, main course, and dessert, all on the move.

The cocktail party—a device for paying off obligations to people you don't want to invite to dinner.

—CHARLES MERRILL SMITH

ugly cheese krispie biscuits 

THESE GROWN-UP Rice Krispie treats are perfect with a gin and tonic at cocktail time. They are very crumbly, but even the crumbs taste great. My grandmother would make us Shirley Temples with these biscuits when we spent the night at her house. Your guests will be all over these biscuits like moles on a grandma.

- **½ cup (1 stick) butter, at room temperature**
- **2 cups grated Cheddar cheese**
- **¾ cup all-purpose flour**
- **Cayenne pepper to taste**
- **Salt to taste**
- **3 cups crisp rice cereal (such as Rice Krispies)**

Preheat the oven to 350°F.

In a mixing bowl, beat the butter with an electric mixer or wooden spoon until fluffy. Add the cheese, flour, cayenne pepper, salt, and cereal and mix well.

Drop the dough by teaspoonfuls onto an ungreased baking sheet, and then flatten the dough with the tines of a fork. Bake for 10 to 15 minutes, until the biscuits are set but not browned. Cool on a wire rack and serve. MAKES **25** TO **30** BISCUITS

SLOB SMARTS

In 1907, the Kellogg company ran a racy promotion campaign with newspaper advertisements that stated, "Give the grocer a wink and see what you get: KTC." KTC stood for Kellogg's Toasted Corn Flakes, and every customer who winked at the grocer received a free cereal sample. In New York sales increased from two railroad carloads a month to a train carload a day!

(Source: *Best Recipes from the Backs of Boxes, Bottles, Cans and Jars* by Ceil Dyer, Galahad Books, New York, 1979.)

cocktail grapes

WHEN YOU SERVE THESE, your friends are going to beg for more! Not because they are particularly tasty, but because they are not very filling. (They are only little grapes with cheese and nuts smushed around them, for crying out loud.)

- **1½ cups herbed cheese spread, such as Boursin**
- **30 large seedless grapes**
- **½ cup finely chopped walnuts**

In a small bowl, beat the cheese with a fork until soft and smooth. Press the cheese around each grape and then roll in the nuts. Refrigerate for at least 30 minutes before serving. SERVES **6**

slob smarts The only time I feel any enthusiasm for housekeeping is when I have friends coming over, but even then I'm not up for a daylong cleaning marathon. I have perfected the "Irish tidy," whereby I run around and shove things in the closet. Set a kitchen timer for 7 minutes, and race around the house, trying to get as much stuff put away in 420 seconds as you can. Even the messiest house can be improved in 7 minutes of frenzied cleaning.

If you need to actually clean, as in scrub, save time and concentrate your efforts on the most conspicuous areas, like the entry hall, the living room, and the guest bathroom. Then dim the lights and spark up some scented candles.

Life is too short to stuff a mushroom.

—SHIRLEY CONRAN, SUPERWOMAN, 1978

god bless american cheese rockets 

THIS EXPLOSIVE COMBINATION of fireworks and *fromage* will liven up the dullest dinners. Skewer cubes of your favorite cheese on the stick end of a bottle rocket (not the dynamite-shaped end filled with gunpowder that shoots flaming balls—definitely not that end!). Light them and watch your guests pursue their hors d'oeuvres around the backyard.

If you happen to live in a state where fireworks are outlawed, or if you prefer cheese without danger, you can create faux cheese rockets. Use real cheese and make fake bottle rockets with construction paper that is rolled and taped onto a wooden skewer or pick. Write your own dramatic warnings on the fake explosives.

Cheese is milk's leap towards immortality.

—CLIFTON FADIMAN

In my wilder days of youth, a group of coworkers were celebrating the birthday of a colleague. Someone went to a swanky bakery and purchased one of those chocolate cakes with a menacing name, like "Death by Chocolate Fudge." We met up in the conference room to fill the void in our empty cubicle careers with cake, and someone noticed that we didn't have candles for the birthday girl. I remembered that I had bought some sparklers in Chinatown during a lunch break, and jigged off to my cubicle to collect them.

We gathered around the cake, inserted the sparklers, and lit them. As we began to sing "Happy Birthday," it became explosively clear that my "sparklers" were combustible bottle rockets as the Roman candle–like fireworks burst into a hissing, fireball shooting, cake-exploding mess. To this day, I swear it was unintentional. Since I learned this lesson for all of us, please serve the cheese rockets alfresco.

slob smarts *Tyrophile* is the term used to describe a cheese aficionado, derived from the Greek "*tyro*" for cheese and phile, meaning "lover of."

buffalo-style shrimp

THIS IS A TWIST on the classic buffalo wings. The shrimp cook in about 2 minutes and there are no bones to gnaw around. They are a cinch to make and go perfectly with margaritas. You will thank me.

4 tablespoons (1/2 stick) butter, melted
3 1/2 tablespoons hot-pepper sauce (like Frank's or Texas Pete's)
1 tablespoon minced garlic
1 pound peeled, deveined jumbo shrimp (approximately 24)
Celery sticks and lime wedges for garnish

Preheat the broiler. Line a baking sheet with foil.

In a small bowl, combine the butter, hot-pepper sauce, and garlic. Place the shrimp on the foil-lined pan and drizzle with one-half of the butter/hot-pepper sauce mixture.

Broil for 1 minute, flip the shrimp, and broil for 1 more minute, until the shrimp are just cooked through.

Toss with the remaining sauce. Arrange in a serving bowl and garnish with lime wedges and celery sticks. SERVES **8**

PREPARTY ANXIETY

Do all the prep you can before your guests arrive; at least half of any culinary success is in the planning.

- **Create a house specialty drink. Guests never know what you have in the bar or what they want to drink. Offering a house drink makes it easy. Pick a favorite and make it your signature. In our home it's a Cuervo Authentic Margarita or a Dark and Stormy (rum, ginger beer, and lime) in the summer and a Milk Punch (page 31) in the winter. Keep the ingredients on hand, as well as beer, and red and white wine.**
- **Stock the bathroom with fresh tissues, towels, soaps, and fresh flowers or a scented candle.**
- **Dim the lights, and light some candles to create a party atmosphere.**
- **Don't neglect the little things, like warmed dinner plates, candles, flowers, and polished silver.**
- **Use a warming tray; even the most precise planning can't predict when all your guests will sit down at the dinner table.**
- **Don't brood over details.**
- **Plan two parties in a row, on successive nights.**
- **Don't be too busy to enjoy your own party.**
- **Ask your best pal to come over a half hour before the rest of the guests are expected, to relax and have a laugh with you before the party kicks off.**

kiss-me-not canapés 

THESE SIMPLE HORS D'OEUVRES are a classic in the leafy enclave of northwestern Connecticut where my husband and I have a farm. They are an old-school, country-club standard that are remarkably tasty and take only minutes to prepare. They will be eaten as fast as you can serve them.

• • •

In a small bowl, mix together 1/2 cup mayonnaise with 1/2 cup freshly grated Parmesan cheese and 1/4 cup chopped onion.

Using a small cookie cutter or shot glass, cut rounds of white bread about 1-inch in diameter. Cover the bread disks with the mayo-cheese-onion mixture and broil for 5 to 7 minutes, until puffed and brown.

slob smarts A swizzle stick or cocktail umbrella can elevate a drink, lift the spirits, and turn your wallflower guest into a lampshade-dancing, one-person conga line.

The only real stumbling block is fear of failure. In cooking you've got to have a what-the-hell attitude.

—JULIA CHILD

bacon and water chestnuts 

rumaki, angels on horseback, whatever you call them

A RIDDLE, a mystery, or an enigma wrapped in crispy bacon.

• • •

For each hors d'oeuvre, wrap a piece of bacon around a water chestnut and skewer with a toothpick. Marinate in 1 cup soy sauce mixed with 1/2 cup brown sugar. Broil until the bacon is crisp, about 3 minutes on each side.

marinated olives 

BUY GOOD OLIVES—black, green, whichever you prefer. Dress them with a drizzle of olive oil, freshly grated lemon or orange zest, and a few flakes of dried red pepper. Extra credit if you warm them gently before serving with cocktails.

slob smarts For big parties, fill your washing machine, bathtub, wheelbarrow, or baby pool with ice and pack it with beverages.

A toast to the cocktail party, where olives are speared and friends are stabbed in the back.

—GROUCHO MARX

feta cheese spread 

MY HUSBAND'S GRANDPARENTS (tyrophiles of the highest order) ate feta cheese at nearly every meal. His grandfather died at age 103 and his grandmother is still full-scream in her ninth decade of life. I can't guarantee that this spread will increase your life span, but it is wonderful on toast.

• • •

In a small bowl, break up about 8 ounces of feta with a fork.
Mix in about 2 tablespoons of olive oil and 1 clove of garlic, minced, until well blended. Serve with hot pita bread for a cocktail snack.
SERVES **4** TO **6**

slob smarts Colorful lanterns and pots of flowers welcome your guests before they cross the threshold.

Garlic is the ketchup of intellectuals.

—ANONYMOUS

cheese crisps

IF EFFICIENCY is intelligent laziness, I'm Albert Einstein, and we all know how much Einstein loved cheese. These are easier to make than falling off a chair.

8 tablespoons freshly grated Parmesan or provolone cheese

Heat a nonstick skillet over medium-high heat. Spoon 1 tablespoon of cheese onto the heated skillet and let it melt and brown lightly, about 2 minutes. Use a spatula to transfer the crisps onto a rack to cool. Repeat 7 times. MAKES **8** CRISPS

slob smarts As host, one should not pour alcohol with the heavy hand of a flirtatious bartender serving a sorority on Ladies' Night. Party responsibly. Also, set up the bar away from your prep area. It will drive you crazy to have your guests drinking and smoking in your work area. They will lean against the refrigerator, crowd you, and piss you off. Do you really want an audience when you fumble the turkey and have to scoop it up off the kitchen floor? Place a bowl of olives or a plate of cheese crisps by the bar to keep them busy and out of your hair.

Age is not important unless you're cheese.

—HELEN HAYES

spiced pecans 

MY FRIEND DAVID buys pecans in bulk and makes these addictive nuts in 5-pound batches. If you eat enough of them, you will bulk up as well. Be careful with the caramelized nuts; the sugar is very hot.

1 tablespoon oil or butter, plus more for the pan
2 cups pecan halves
½ cup sugar
1 teaspoon salt
1 teaspoon cayenne pepper
¼ teaspoon cinnamon

Lightly oil a baking dish or brownie pan.

In a large skillet, heat the tablespoon of oil or butter over medium heat. Add the pecan halves and toss for 2 or 3 minutes to toast. Add the sugar and continue cooking until the sugar caramelizes. Pour the nuts out onto the prepared baking dish, in one layer, and toss with the salt, cayenne pepper, and cinnamon. MAKES **2** CUPS

slob smarts Hang a small mirror on the inside of your pantry, as that's most likely where you will be when the doorbell rings. That way you can check your face so you won't get busted with chocolate icing on your nose.

At a dinner party one should eat wisely
but not too well,
and speak well but not too wisely.

—W. SOMERSET MAUGHAM

salty, warm nuts 

THESE NUTS are first-class.

• • •

In a large skillet, melt 2 tablespoons of butter over medium heat. Toss in 2 cups of nuts (pecans or almonds), season with salt, and stir until thoroughly warmed, about 4 minutes. MAKES **2** CUPS

sticky chicken wings 

I SERVED THESE tasty wings the night I hosted our book club. You should have seen the smeared, sticky pages; we made a mess. I would skip these if you are hosting a quilting bee or a card party. A nice touch would be to dampen some washcloths with water and a little lemon juice and warm them in the microwave. Toss these to your guests with the sticky wings.

- **½ cup honey**
- **½ cup teriyaki sauce**
- **4 pounds chicken wings, trimmed (approximately 25 wings)**

Preheat the oven to 400°F.

In a resealable plastic bag, combine the honey and teriyaki sauce and mix well. Toss in the wings and marinate in the refrigerator for at least 1 hour.

Pour the chicken and marinade into a 9 × 13-inch pan and bake for 25 minutes. Flip the wings and bake for another 20 minutes, until browned, crispy, and sticky. SERVES **4** TO **6**

slob smarts The most important ingredient for a party is your guest list.

girls' club crab dip 

MY MOTHER AND A GROUP OF HER FRIENDS have been meeting every other Tuesday night for forty-four years. They call themselves The Girls' Club. The twelve original members have shared every triumph and tragedy. If one divorces, they hold a divorce shower. If one loses a spouse, the others are there all night to comfort and console. My father believes this group has saved its members millions in therapy bills.

They meet at one another's houses, each taking the hostess duty twice a year. One of the fondest recollections of my childhood is sitting at the top of the stairs with my sisters, listening to my mom and her friends crack one another up. We also loved getting to eat the leftovers the next day.

- 1 8-ounce package of Neufchâtel or cream cheese, softened
- 1 6-ounce can white crab meat
- 1/4 cup mayonnaise
- 1 tablespoon chopped onion
- 1 teaspoon mustard
- 1 teaspoon Worcestershire sauce
- Dash of paprika

Preheat the oven to 350°F.

In a 9-inch pie plate, mix the Neufchâtel cheese, crab meat, mayonnaise, onion, mustard, and Worcestershire sauce. Bake for 15 to 20 minutes, until bubbly. Garnish with paprika and serve with crackers. MAKES **2** CUPS

slob smarts The host almost always misses the party, unless she plans it in advance. Outline the party on paper, and include a timeline. Set your table and do most of your cooking before your guests arrive; schedule time to get dressed, groomed, and relaxed. My husband's grandparents started the tradition of "the Psychological Cocktail." It is the drink you enjoy with your spouse or best friend before your guests arrive.

hummus

HUMMUS, THE UBIQUITOUS NECTAR spread liberally at hairy-legged, sprout-crunching health-food shops, is high in fiber and very easy to make on your own. Of course, you could buy the commercially prepared stuff for ten times the price. It's your money; I'm not the boss of you.

- **1 15-ounce can garbanzo beans (chickpeas), drained and rinsed**
- **Juice of 1 lemon**
- **1 tablespoon olive oil, plus more for serving**
- **1 garlic clove, minced**
- **Ground cumin to taste**
- **Parsley flakes to taste**
- **Cayenne pepper to taste**
- **Salt and pepper to taste**

In a medium bowl, mash the garbanzo beans, lemon juice, olive oil, and garlic with a potato masher until smooth. (It will take a few minutes, and if you get tired, you can call it "chunky style" hummus.)

It is okay now, but taste it, and add a few shakes of cumin and parsley flakes, and a dash of cayenne, salt, and pepper. Pour a few more teaspoons of oil over the top and mix well.

Serve with pita chips, crackers, or carrots sticks.

MAKES A SCANT **2** CUPS

slob smarts Keep a dictionary in the dining room; this is where all the good conversations take place and interesting questions are asked.

slob salsa

To make a jar of store-bought salsa seem homemade, stir in a bit of chopped onion, some chopped cilantro, and a squeeze of fresh lime juice. Place wedges of lime around the salsa bowl.

slob smarts Make mix CDs for your party. They free you from having to be the DJ on top of all your other host duties. Be sure that the volume does not interfere with conversation.

tequila lime ceviche

If you don't feel like cooking, take a crack at this fresh-tasting ceviche, which cooks in citrus juice and premixed margaritas for a bit of a kick. If you want to skip the alcohol entirely, just use margarita mix.

- **1 pound fresh scallops or peeled, deveined shrimp**
- **1 small red onion, chopped**
- **¼ cup Jose Cuervo Authentic Margaritas in classic lime**
- **1 cup fresh lime juice (reserve juiced lime halves for serving)**
- **¼ teaspoon red hot pepper flakes**
- **3 tablespoons olive oil**
- **Salt and pepper**

In a glass bowl, combine the fresh scallops, onion, margaritas, and ½ cup of the fresh lime juice. Cover and refrigerate for 4 hours.

Drain the seafood and onions, then combine with the remaining ½ cup of fresh lime juice, the olive oil, and salt and pepper to taste. Spoon into the juiced lime halves or a martini glass and serve immediately. SERVES **4**

fiesta like there is no mañana guacamole

THIS IS BEST if you serve it immediately after preparing it. If you need to hold it for an hour or so, place an avocado pit in the dip and cover the whole bowl with plastic wrap. The pit will keep the guacamole from discoloring.

- 1 tablespoon kosher salt
- 5 garlic cloves, peeled and smashed
- 3 large ripe avocados
- 5 tablespoons fresh lime juice

Sprinkle the salt on a wooden cutting board and mince the garlic with the salt to make a paste.

Cut the avocados in half, remove the pits, and scoop the flesh into a bowl. Mash the avocados with a fork, then stir in the lime juice and the garlic/salt paste. MAKES ABOUT **2** CUPS, DEPENDING ON THE SIZE OF THE AVOCADOS

slob smarts For a party, serve this guacamole in a sombrero. Turn the sombrero upside down, and place the serving bowl of guacamole in the crown. Fill the brim with tortilla chips.

retro slob smarts

Reserve avocado pits when making guacamole. Hold the pit with the large end on the bottom, and push three toothpicks into the pit about a third of the way from the bottom. Suspend the pit in a glass jar, and fill the jar with water to cover the pit about an inch. Keep adding water so that 1 inch of the pit is submerged. Small roots will begin to grow from the bottom and a stem from the top. After about 3 weeks, remove the toothpicks and transfer the pit into a clay pot with potting soil.

cheese and wine

WHEN YOUR FRIENDS are swinging by to see you, don't act as if they're health inspectors on red alert for kitchen violations. A simple selection of cheeses and a nice bottle of wine are just fine as refreshments. Here are a few rules of thumb to assist you in hosting a casual wine and cheese get-together:

- For a wine and cheese party, allow one pound of cheese for every five guests.
- A standard wine bottle holds six glasses of wine.
- When creating a cheese plate, choose at least three kinds of cheese. (That includes the kind that sprays out of a can.) Vary them by texture, taste, and type of milk—sheep, goat, or cow.
- Creamy, high-fat cheeses, like Brie, Explorateur, and Saint-André, go best with white wine. Offer both red and white wines, and have fun experimenting with what tastes best together.
- To store hard cheeses, wrap them in wax paper, then foil or loose plastic wrap.
- Wrap cheeses like Brie tightly in plastic to prevent them from oozing all over. The harder the cheese, the longer it lasts.
- Let cheese sit at room temperature for two hours before your guests arrive. Coldness mutes the flavor of cheese.
- Use different knives to slice each cheese, so the flavors don't get mixed up.
- Supplement the cheese and fruit plates with nuts, raw vegetables, and some smoked meat.

egg cream

I GAVE my four-year-old godson the complete collection of *Little Rascals* on DVD, an eighty-hour compilation of the best of Spanky, Alfalfa, Buckwheat, Stymie, Miss Crabtree, Mr. Hood, Petey, and the gang. He promply developed his first obsession, asking his mom for a pair of plaid knickers, just like Spanky wore, and requesting a "wheep whomp surprise cake" for his fifth birthday. Most startling, he has adopted the speech pattern and vocabulary of a hambone vaudevillian from eight decades ago. He can repeat dialogue at length, like the "Don't drink the milk" bit, and recite the soliloquy about having to eat mush. When one afternoon he said, "Listen, sister—what do you say if we hotfoot it outta here and we spring for an egg cream," I nearly burst with pride.

Milk
Chocolate or vanilla syrup
Seltzer water

Fill a tall glass a quarter full with milk. Stir in chocolate or vanilla syrup, and fill the glass with seltzer (preferably spritzed from a syphon). The foamy froth resembles beaten egg whites. SERVES **1**

The correct order of beverages is starting with the most temperate and ending with the most heady.

—JEAN-ANTHELME BRILLAT-SAVARIN,
THE PHYSIOLOGY OF TASTE, 1825

lemonade

One summer afternoon, I was fixing sandwiches and lemonade for my nieces and nephew. While I was strapping the youngest baby into her high chair I asked the little munchkin if she could talk. “Not yet,” she replied.

If you are going to make lemonade, either for yourself, or for an enterprising six-year-old’s stand, make *real* lemonade, from lemons.

1½ cups lemon juice, freshly squeezed from 8 large lemons
½ cup sugar, or more or less to taste
1 teaspoon vanilla extract
5 cups cold water
1 large lemon, cut into small wedges or thin cartwheel slices

In a large pitcher, mix the lemon juice, sugar, vanilla, and the water and stir to dissolve the sugar. Garnish each glass with a wedge or slice of lemon. SERVES **6**

We are living in an age where
furniture polish is made with real lemons
and lemonade is made with artificial lemons.

—ALFRED E. NEWMAN (MAD MAGAZINE)

hot mexican coffee 

I LOVE TO SERVE Irish or Mexican coffee in the winter months. I make my own coffee liqueur (see page 33), but the stuff you brought back from your cruise to Cancún is fine.

- 1/2 cup coffee liqueur, such as Kahlúa
- 3 1/2 cups brewed coffee
- Whipped cream
- 2 tablespoons sugar (optional)

Add a shot of coffee liqueur to a cup of hot coffee, and top with whipped cream.

For extra credit, moisten the rim of the coffee mug with a bit of coffee liqueur and then dip in sugar, the way you serve a salted margarita. SERVES **4**

slob smarts Hiccup Cures: Having someone hold your ears while you drink a glass of water, or swallowing a teaspoon of sugar, are a couple of the traditional methods of curing hiccups. Another is to name three bald men in quick succession.

Alcohol is a misunderstood vitamin.

—P. G. WODEHOUSE

Behind every successful woman . . . is a substantial amount of coffee.

—STEPHANIE PIRO

milk punch

THIS IS WHAT we serve at the annual New Year's Day skating party we host on our pond. Watching fifty hungover adults sliding around the pond is a vision; this is their reward for making it across.

- **1 jigger bourbon**
- **1 tablespoon pure maple syrup**
- **2/3 cup hot or cold milk**
- **Fresh nutmeg**

In a tumbler, mix together the bourbon and maple syrup. Add the milk. Top with fresh nutmeg shavings. SERVES **1**

slob smarts Connecticut is known as the nutmeg state, although nutmeg is not cultivated within a thousand miles of the state. In colonial times, hucksters carved wooden ovals in the shape of nutmeg and sold them off as the precious tropical spice. Connecticut is called the nutmeg state meaning that you won't get a fair shake from the residents, known as nutmeggers.

3 wise men

- **1 shot Jack Daniel's**
- **1 shot Jim Beam**
- **1 shot Johnnie Walker**

Combine the shots and drink. SERVES **1**

Kipling said,
"It is no time for mirth and laughter,
that cold grey dawn of the morning after."

jell-o shots

MODERN IMMATURITY at its zenith! My husband and I served these at our wedding party, and we also had a kissing booth. This combustible combination was a smash success with our guests and made for some memorable family photos.

1 small package lime Jell-O
3 cups boiling water
1 cup vodka

In a large measuring bowl with a spout, add the Jell-O and the boiling water, and stir. Let the mixture rest for one minute, then stir in the vodka. Pour into small paper cups, and refrigerate for 4 hours, or until firm. MAKES **16** SHOTS

slob smarts The best way to treat a hangover is to drink lots of water, take aspirin, and sleep it off. Some believe in the restorative powers of the hair of the dog, or even an entire coat!

The difficulty lies not in the use of a bad thing but in the abuse of a very good thing.

—ABRAHAM LINCOLN

homemade coffee liqueur 

I BECAME inspired to make homemade coffee liqueur when my friend Paula Polite gave me a cookbook published by the Memphis Junior League. In a frenzy of domestic enthusiasm I whipped up a double batch. I had gallons of it curing in my laundry room. My husband teased me about being a bootlegger and distilling the sweet sorority-girl booze. I made so much I was decanting it into mason jars, like the two spinster sisters with the "recipe" on *The Waltons,* and giving it to friends. Now they request it.

- **6 cups sugar**
- **6 tablespoons plus 2 teaspoons instant coffee**
- **1/2 gallon vodka**
- **1/4 cup pure vanilla extract**

In a large saucepan, mix the sugar, 6 cups of water, and the coffee and bring to slow boil. Reduce the heat and simmer for 1 hour.

Remove from the heat and cover the saucepan with a lid. Let sit for 12 hours. Add the vodka and vanilla and stir well. Pour the liquid into dark bottles. Let sit for 30 days for best results. MAKES **3** QUARTS

be a good guest

GOOD MANNERS can get you anywhere in life. The etiquette of entertaining begins with a code of behavior based on kindness and consideration. It continues with guidelines that enable you to be self-confident and comfortable in any situation. By the same token, a good guest is enthusiastic and considerate and treats his or her host and fellow guests with thoughtfulness and respect. Sadly, one can't count on every guest to adhere to this code. For those that don't, I have instituted the Don't Let the Door Hit You in the Ass Awards, with several categories.

THE WHINER

If you are not feeling well, don't talk about it. Suck it up for the host and the other guests, or stay home. I remember a visit from one friend to our farm. This guy, whom I'll call BFB (Big Fat Baby), was one of fifteen guests invited for the weekend. It was a full house, and I was busy and having fun with my friends. Well, Mr. BFB decided that he didn't feel well, and he bored us to tears with his moaning at the dinner table. He then bolted down his dinner like a hound and left the dining room. When he didn't return, I excused myself and went looking for him.

I found the bum stretched out on the couch in the library, watching TV. If he was so sick, I suggested, perhaps he should jig upstairs to his room, as we had fourteen other perfectly lovely guests to consider and a long night of music and dancing ahead of us. An engaged TV sucks the life out of a room.

Would you like some cheese with that whine?

Sometimes there is nothing like a knucklehead to galvanize a group. The crybaby spent the night sulking while we danced and pulled out our basket of percussion instruments and played along with the music until four A.M. The rest of us wound up having a wickedly fun weekend, and he had to wait until Sunday to get a ride back to the city. After that weekend I weeded my social garden and dropped him cold. So, if you have a tendency to be a whiny crybaby, don't accept invitations.

THE BOOZY SUZIE

We invited two couples over for a small dinner party at our home. I made a beautiful leg of lamb and put time and thought into creating a lovely dinner for six. It should have been great, but one of our guests dominated the conversation and rudely interrupted the other guests. The wine had loosened her tongue, so much so that we all wanted to rip it out. My plan was to have everyone finish their dinner, and then move to the living room to have some homemade baked Alaska by the fire. But before the other guests had finished their salad, the schnockered saucepan got up from the table. She stumbled back into the dining room carrying the basket of brownies I had baked for an elderly neighbor. "Look what I found," she slurred. Returning to her chair, she placed the basket on top of her dirty dinner plate, and shoveled every single brownie into her pie hole. Again, not someone who will be eating chez moi again soon.

MONSTER CHILDREN

If you and your family are guests, remember that good manners apply to people of all ages. Friends came over with their two small boys, ginger-haired little beasts who ripped our houseplants out by the roots, sprayed Pam cooking spray on the walls like two-foot-tall vandals, and tormented our family pet. When I grabbed the can of spray oil from their tiny greasy meat hooks and told them to knock it off, their parents sternly told me not to discipline their children.

The uncivilized little cretins nicked my wallet from my bedroom, climbed on my furniture with dirty sneakers, and ate sticky peanut butter and jelly sandwiches in our living room. It was exhausting. The parents allowed their children to disrespect our home—but only once.

If you have a tale of a memorably awful guest, he or she could be the recipient of the First Annual Slob in the Kitchen Don't Let the Door Hit You in the Ass Award. Send your story of houseguest from hell to www.slobinthekitchen.com, and we will vote for a winner.

First prize is a certificate, suitable for framing.

I live on good soup, not on fine words.

—MOLIÈRE

crackpot

improve your

culinary reputation

with a pot of soup or stew

WHEN DINING OUT, my husband always orders soup. When I asked him why, he explained, **"Soup is usually good, it's hard to screw up, and it's something I don't often eat at home."**

I figured that if simpletons have been making pots of soup for thousands of years, I might as well take a crack at it. **A grown-up shouldn't be intimidated by a soup recipe** (or by anything else, for that matter), so I bought a cookbook specializing in soups and got on with it. The result is that I am now an enthusiastic soup maker, and my favorites are adapted for this chapter.

There are several kinds of soups: thin broths and consommés; soups that have been thickened by the addition of a starch like potatoes, pasta, rice, beans, or flour; soups that have been enriched with egg yolks; and my favorites, soups that have been puréed. I highly recommend an immersion stick blender for this procedure; **pouring hot soup from a pot into a blender and then back into the pot again is a round-trip I want to avoid.** Crack open your wallet, and purchase a $20 immersion blender. It will transform your soup-making skills.

Don't be pushed around by cookbook authors who insist that you roast up a carcass in order to make soup. **I would never in a million years suggest that you brew your own stock.** (I don't know about you, but I prefer my soup making without the Hannibal Lechter gore.) Poke around in gourmet shops and swanky food aisles for the best soup bases, stocks, and broths. My favorites are in paste concentrate form, sold in costly, stout little jars, but some canned varieties are acceptable. **Since you are going out of your way to make soup, you might as well start off with the good stuff.** If, however, you are snowbound, or quarantined, or under house arrest, bouillon cubes can be used in a moment of soup desperation.

Soupmaking doesn't require much culinary heavy lifting. For a simple vegetable soup, the steps are quite simple:

1. Sauté finely chopped aromatic vegetables (celery, onions, leeks, and the like) in fat in a pot.
2. Add stock to the pot.
3. Simmer the vegetables in the stock until tender, then serve chunky style or purée.

The results will far outshine the canned stuff that Mom used to heat up. That stated, there are always exceptions, and the quick-fix recipe for doctored-up condensed tomato soup that follows can be prepared in the time it takes to toast the bread. I got hooked on it during the meatless Fridays of Lent, and now I serve it for Saturday lunch all year 'round.

In taking soup, it is necessary to avoid lifting too much in the spoon, or filling the mouth so full as almost to stop the breath.

—ST. JOHN THE BAPTIST DE LA SALLE

white bean and pesto soup 

I FOUND THIS HANDWRITTEN RECIPE taped into the front cover of a cookbook I picked up at a library sale. I make it all the time; it's my husband's favorite. I had him believing that I donned an apron and spent hours in the kitchen; now he'll know how simple it is.

- **2 cups chicken broth or stock**
- **2 19-ounce cans white beans, drained and rinsed**
- **2 tablespoons pesto sauce**
- **2 tablespoons grated Parmesan cheese**

In a saucepan, bring the chicken stock to a boil.

Add the white beans and simmer for 2 minutes, then stir in the pesto and Parmesan. SERVES **4**

red devil

MY FAVORITE GRANDMOTHER would throw this together in five minutes and serve it to her grandchildren. I remember her snapping, "Let's get cracking. The only person who ever got all their housework done by Friday was Robinson Crusoe." A day doesn't go by that I don't miss her.

- **1 can condensed tomato soup**
- **½ cup milk**
- **1 cup shredded Cheddar cheese**
- **1 teaspoon Worcestershire sauce**
- **8 slices buttered toast, cut into triangles**

In a saucepan, stir together the soup, milk, cheese, and Worcestershire sauce over medium-high heat until the cheese is melted.

Spoon the red devil mixture over toast triangles. SERVES **4**

carrot soup

MY FRIEND AND COOKING TEACHER Miss Beverly Morris taught me this recipe, which is my favorite soup. I never tire of making it and I never tire of eating it. If you are a soup novice, sharpen your skills and stir up a pot. Miss Beverly toasts slices of buttered French bread and floats one in each bowl of soup.

Food processors seem slightly sinister to me; the scalpel–sharp razors whirring about like mad just look like trouble. Plus they take up valuable counter space and are harder to clean than a knife and a cutting board. If I feel like making carrot soup, I'll take a few minutes to chop the carrots or use a few bags of baby carrots rather than drag out a heavy appliance. I double and triple this recipe and freeze it in 2-cup portions.

4 tablespoons (½ stick) butter
1 cup chopped onion
12 large carrots, peeled and chopped, or 2 1-pound bags of peeled baby carrots
2 or 3 celery stalks (optional)
4 cups chicken stock

In a large pot, melt the butter. Toss in the onion and cook over low heat, stirring occasionally, until tender and translucent. Add the carrots and celery, if using, and cook, stirring occasionally, for 5 minutes.

Pour in the stock and bring to a boil. Reduce the heat to low, cover, and simmer until the carrots are tender, about 30 minutes.

Using a stick immersion blender, purée the soup right in the pot, until smooth. SERVES **6**

slob smarts The ladies of the court of France's Louis XI subsisted mainly on soup because they believed chewing would cause them to develop wrinkles.

greek lemon soup

HIPPOCRATES SAID, "Let food be your medicine." When I was going through chemo, my husband's Greek grandmother would make this soup for me, and it did make me feel better.

- 8 cups chicken stock
- ½ cup uncooked rice
- 4 eggs
- Juice of 2 lemons

In a large saucepan, bring the stock to a boil. Add the rice and simmer for 20 minutes.

Just before serving, in a large mixing bowl beat the eggs until they are light and foamy. Beat in the lemon juice and about 2 cups of the hot soup. Beat the egg-lemon mixture into the remaining hot soup over low heat. Do not boil; if it boils, the eggs will cook through and the soup will lose its frothy texture.

Garnish each bowl with 2 thin slices of lemon. SERVES **8**

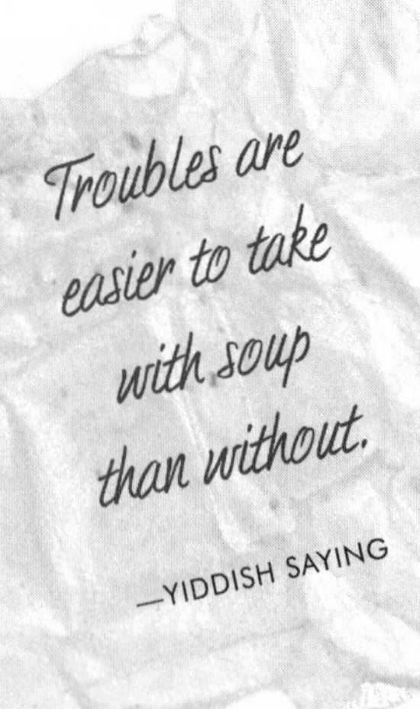

fix-you-right-up soup 

IN THE TWELFTH CENTURY physician and philosopher Moses Maimonides praised chicken soup's medicinal properties, and medical research in recent years has proven chicken soup's superiority to other hot liquids. The tests supporting the efficacy of chicken soup as a cold remedy were so impressive that a Florida hospital began to package and sell its own brand of chicken soup.

This is perfect for the morning after you've had too much loudmouth soup (booze). It's so easy and virtuous, you'll be back up and ready to go, fortified for another big night out, before you know it.

4 cups of the best chicken broth you can find without having to make it yourself
1 tablespoon minced garlic (or as much as you can stand)
Juice of 1 lemon

In a saucepan, simmer the chicken broth and garlic together until steaming hot.

Stir in the lemon juice, and serve with buttered toast. SERVES **4**

slob smarts Homemade croutons elevate a simple soup into something special. The Ugly Cheese Krispie Biscuits (page 12) or Beer Bread (page 191) are great options for croutons. Preheat the oven to 400°F. Pour a bit of olive oil in a bowl, toss in some bread cut into 1-inch cubes, and add seasoning to taste. Spread the oiled bread bits on a baking sheet and toast in the oven for 8 to 10 minutes, until brown and crunchy.

summer roasted tomato soup 

To eat ripe seasonal tomatoes is to taste perfection. Take it from this Jersey Tomato who grew up in the Garden State: The lush taste of a sun-warmed tomato is vastly superior to the flaccid, empty taste of one out of season. My favorite summer sandwich is sliced tomato sprinkled with sea salt on squishy white bread.

Make this recipe when you have an abundance of red, ripe tomatoes; otherwise, try the winter version of this recipe on the next page.

• • •

Toss a few pounds of tomatoes, cored and sliced into wedges, with a liberal amount of olive oil. Add some chopped garlic and a sprinkling of fresh thyme and rosemary. Place in a roasting pan in a 400°F. oven for about 45 minutes, stirring halfway through. When the tomatoes break down, the garlic is soft, and the dish smells divine, it's done. Remove from the oven.

In a heavy stockpot, sauté a minced red onion in olive oil until translucent. Then add the roasted tomatoes to the pot. Cover with 6 cups of chicken stock or vegetable stock. Bring to a boil, then reduce the heat and simmer over low heat, stirring occasionally, for 5 minutes. With an immersion stick blender, purée the soup, giving it a series of pulses to pulverize the tomatoes and break down the skins and seeds. SERVES **6**

Hearing a good loud soup is very enjoyable.

—BERT MILTON

winter roasted tomato soup 

JUST SO YOU KNOW, once a soup has gone wrong anything you might add to rescue it will only make it worse. This is a simple soup, so don't monkey with it too much; the beauty is in its simplicity.

- 1 28-ounce can of tomatoes, whole or chopped, drained
- 2 garlic cloves, chopped
- Fresh rosemary to taste
- Fresh thyme to taste
- Olive oil
- 1 medium red onion, minced
- 4 cups chicken stock or vegetable stock
- 1 cup heavy cream (optional)

Place the drained tomatoes, garlic, rosemary, and thyme in a baking dish, splash with oil, and roast at 400°F. for 30 minutes, stirring halfway through.

In a stockpot, heat some more olive oil and sauté the onion. Add the tomato mixture and cover with the stock. Bring to a boil, then reduce to a simmer, stirring occasionally, for 5 more minutes. If you felt like cream of roasted tomato soup, now would be the time to gently stir in the cup of heavy cream.

You can serve it like this, chunky style, or purée it—whatever you feel like. SERVES **6**

slob smarts Always wash the top of a can before opening it. Many grocers spray the shelves with pesticides.

Make a good soup, a distinctive soup,
a soup your friends can rely upon, and you're a chef.

—*ESQUIRE HANDBOOK FOR HOSTS*, 1999

chicken lime soup with tortillas 

THIS IS A FLAVORFUL TWIST on the traditional chicken noodle soup—and you will be in and out of the kitchen in two shakes of a maraca.

- 1½ pounds boneless chicken breasts
- 2 tablespoons olive oil
- 1 large onion, chopped
- 2 garlic cloves, chopped
- 4 carrots, peeled and chopped into ½-inch slices
- 4 celery stalks, cut into ½-inch slices
- 2 cups chicken stock
- Juice of 1 lime
- 6 corn tortillas, cut into ¼-inch ribbons
- Lime wedges to garnish

Place the chicken breasts in a large saucepan. Cover with water, and bring to a simmer. Cover and cook gently for 10 minutes, or until cooked through. Place on a plate to cool.

In a large soup pot, heat the oil over medium heat and sauté the onion until tender, about 5 minutes. Add the garlic, carrots, and celery and stir, then cover for 5 more minutes. Add the chicken stock to the pot and simmer until the carrots and celery are tender.

Shred the chicken into strips and add to the pot. Add the lime juice.

Ladle into bowls, and toss in a handful of tortilla strips.

Serve with lime wedges. SERVES **8**

But I always felt that I'd rather be a provincial hot tamale than soup without seasoning.

—F. SCOTT FITZGERALD, *THIS SIDE OF PARADISE*, 1920

new england clam chowder 

MANHATTAN CLAM CHOWDER is made with a tomato base and New England clam chowder is made with a cream base. The rivalry between the two is legendary; indeed, the Maine legislature passed a bill in 1939 outlawing the addition of tomatoes to clam chowder. This version should keep you out of the pokey, where you would be someone's prison bitch and get traded for a pack of Kools.

- 3 slices bacon, diced
- 1 potato, diced (2 cups)
- 1/4 cup chopped onion
- 1 6-ounce bottle clam juice
- 1 6-ounce can clams, drained (reserve the juice for the soup broth)
- 2 cups heavy cream
- 4 tablespoons (1/2 stick) butter

In a medium saucepan, brown the bacon; do not drain. Add the potato and onion and sauté for about 7 minutes, until golden.

Add the bottled clam juice and the reserved juice from the drained clams. Cover the pot and simmer for about 10 minutes, until the potato is soft. Reduce the heat to low.

Add the clams, then stir in the cream until blended. Serve with a knob of butter on top of each bowl, to enrich the flavor. SERVES **4**

slob smarts Americans consume more than 10 billion bowls of soup each year.

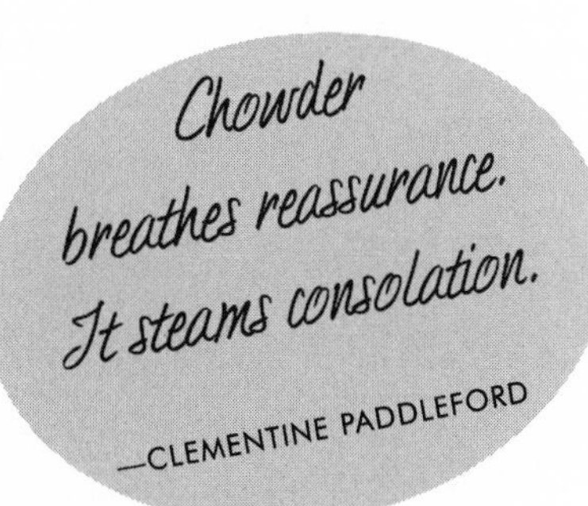

lazy boots beef bourguignon 

I HAVE MADE OCEANS OF BEEF BOURGUIGNON, using recipes from exhaustive books on French cookery to one copied from *Woman* magazine in which canned cream of mushroom soup is a key ingredient.

This recipe is a result of six years of trial and error, and my husband ate every attempt. I can't believe it took so long to figure out an uncomplicated recipe, but I do believe it was worth the wait.

- 4 slices bacon
- 2 pounds cubed beef
- 1 cup tiny white pearl onions, peeled, or 1 large onion, chopped
- 4 garlic cloves, minced
- 2 cups dry red wine
- 2 cups vegetable stock
- 1 cup sliced mushrooms
- Chopped fresh flat-leaf parsley, for garnish

In a large Dutch oven or stew pot, fry the bacon until crisp. Reserve the bacon drippings in the pot and crumble the bacon. Set aside.

Brown the cubed beef in the bacon drippings, then add the onions and garlic and cook until tender.

Add the wine, stock, mushrooms, and crumbled bacon to the pot. Cover and cook over medium-high heat for 1 hour, or until the meat is tender. Serve over buttered noodles and garnish with the parsley.

SERVES **6**

Talk of joy: There may be things better than beef stew and baked potatoes and home-made bread—there may be.

—DAVID GRAYSON

ratatouille vegetable stew 

THIS IS A GREAT DISH to make in bulk. Since you are already in the game, why not double the stew recipe? It doesn't take twice as long to make twelve servings as it does to make six. This way, you only have one set of utensils to wash and you will have the pleasure of knowing that you have a full meal waiting for you in the refrigerator. The flavors will only deepen and improve.

- **½ cup olive oil**
- **1 small onion, sliced**
- **3 medium eggplants, diced (about 3½ cups)**
- **6 tomatoes, peeled and sliced, or 1 28-ounce can of plum tomatoes, drained**
- **2 medium zucchini, sliced**
- **2 green peppers, seeded and chopped**
- **4 garlic cloves, minced**
- **1 tablespoon fresh thyme or ½ teaspoon dried**
- **Salt and pepper**

In a deep, heavy-bottomed skillet or enamel pot, heat the oil over medium-high heat. Sauté the onion until lightly browned. Add the eggplant and cook for about 3 minutes, until slightly softened. Then stir in the tomatoes, zucchini, peppers, and garlic until well mixed. Season with the thyme, salt, and pepper.

Cover and reduce the heat to low. Simmer, stirring frequently, for 20 minutes. Serve hot or cold. SERVES **6**

I don't make soup, it makes itself from what is growing in the garden at the time.

—HELEN NEARING, *SIMPLE FOOD FOR THE GOOD LIFE,* 1980

welsh rarebit

I LOVE COOKING WITH BEER; sometimes I even put it in the food.

4 slices bread, crust trimmed
Butter
1 pound Cheddar cheese, shredded
1 cup beer
Dash of dry mustard
Pinch of cayenne pepper
Pinch of paprika
1 teaspoon Worcestershire sauce
Salt and pepper to taste

Toast and butter the bread.

In a nonstick pan, melt the cheese over medium-low heat. When the cheese is almost melted, add the beer and stir well. Add the mustard, cayenne, paprika, and Worcestershire sauce.

Remove from the heat, pour over the toast, and season with salt and pepper. SERVES **4**

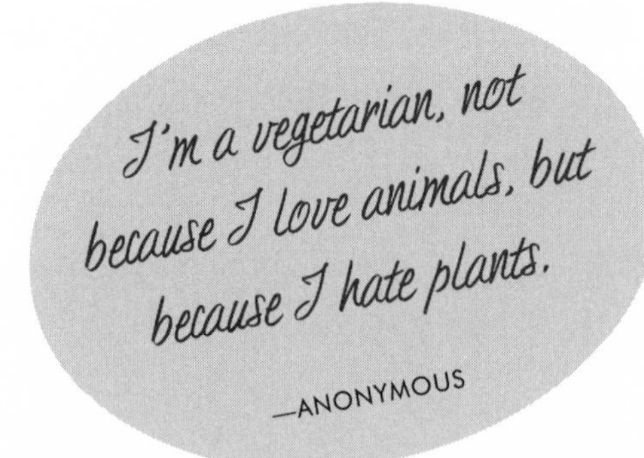

cheat's pea soup 

I SPENT THREE YEARS trying to locate a copy of Lady Caroline Blackwood's cookbook of outrageous cheats called *Darling, You Shouldn't Have Gone to So Much Trouble.* I was directed to a copy by my late friend Mr. George Plimpton.

George offered me his recipe for serving canned Dinty Moore Stew, dressed up with celery stalks and carrots planted upright like a forest in the serving bowl. Mr. Plimpton was famous for many achievements, but the stew recipe is not one of them. Still, he said if I published his recipe, he would let me borrow his copy of Lady Caroline's book. So, I'm keeping up my end of the bargain. Just pretend that you never read George Plimpton's recipe, because the one I found in Lady Caroline's book for Cheat's Pea Soup is so good, it cancels out the tinned stew.

Toasted, buttery croutons liven up most soups. It takes only a few minutes to fry up diced bread in a bit of butter and garlic. Since you'll probably still serve soup from a can once in a while, frying fresh croutons is the least you can do.

1 10-ounce package frozen peas
2 cups chicken stock
4 to 6 fresh mint leaves, or ½ teaspoon dried mint leaves, plus fresh mint leaves for garnish
Sour cream

In a medium saucepan, simmer the peas in the chicken stock until heated thoroughly. Add the mint leaves or dried mint.

With an immersion blender, whiz the mixture up until smooth (it will be thick). Serve hot or cold, with a big spoonful of sour cream and a sprinkle of additional mint. SERVES **4**

cool summer soup 

CHILLED SOUPS are fine as a first course in warm weather. This could not be easier, it tastes great, and it sounds like it would be good for you.

- 1 pint plain yogurt
- 2 cups tomato juice or vegetable juice blend
- Juice and grated zest of 1 orange
- Fresh mint leaves

In a large bowl, whisk together the yogurt and the juices until well blended. Garnish with a pinch of zest and a few mint leaves.

SERVES **4**

Cold soup is a very tricky thing and it is the rare hostess who can carry it off. More often than not the dinner guest is left with the impression that had he only come a little earlier he could have gotten it while it was still hot.

—FRAN LEBOWITZ

scrappy gazpacho

I BREAK MY OWN RULE about not using a blender or food processor for this recipe. Since this is a cold soup, I figure it is safe to give it a go. The sum of these humble ingredients equals a remarkably good bowl of soup. I made it for a Spanish friend who lives on gazpacho and tricked him into thinking I had actually slaved over it. Sucker.

1 quart tomato-vegetable juice (such as V8)
A few slices of French bread, torn into pieces
1 8-ounce jar salsa
Olive oil
1 lemon, thinly sliced

Pour about 1¼ cups of the tomato-vegetable juice into a blender. Toss in the bread, and purée until it breaks down and thickens the juice.

Transfer the puréed bread mixture into a large bowl and add the remaining juice. Stir in the salsa. Chill, covered, in the refrigerator for at least an hour.

Serve cool, enriched with a tiny drizzle of olive oil, and float a thin slice of lemon on top. SERVES **4**

Of soup and love, the first is best.

—SPANISH PROVERB

dress me up, toss me 'round

the world is a salad

and we can all

contribute a leaf

I **HAVE READ** that the most important step in making a great salad is to dry the lettuce leaves thoroughly. **A salad spinner takes up too much space in my claustrophobically tiny kitchen,** so I never bother with one. My friend Beautiful Jenny taught me a few tricks, though, and the printable one is to load the damp leaves in a fresh cotton pillowcase and swing it around your head. Sometimes I just take the leaves from a colander, spread them out on a fresh dish towel, and gently roll it up. (I'm a bit of an environmental tightwad and feel bad about using too many paper towels. How many trees must be pulped for my salad?)

I have also learned a lot from Peg Bracken. I cleave to her *Complete I Hate to Cook Book* as if it is the Ark of the Covenant. Ms. Bracken suggests that if you "fatigue" the lettuce, meaning if **you add a few drops of oil to the washed and dried lettuce leaves, the**

salad dressing will not slide off the leaves. I was somewhat reluctant to believe this, but Ms. Bracken has never misguided me. When we were on vacation with a group of friends and we made big communal dinners, I "fatigued" the lettuce and was the recipient of energetic praise for the resultant salad.

Another trick to making an excellent salad is to use a wooden bowl; it is worth the expense. The daily anointings of olive oil and rubbings of cut garlic cloves will lend a pronounced fragrance to the bowl and flavor to your dressing.

Designer lettuce leaves, triple washed and ready to dress, are a slob's best friend. If you trick them out with hard-boiled eggs, cheese, nuts, fish, beef, or chicken, you can prepare a perfect light meal in moments. Store-bought croutons are repulsively flavored, molar-challenging mockeries; slices of fresh French or Italian bread, toasted, then rubbed with a cut clove of garlic and misted with olive oil, are the recommended salad accompaniment.

carrot and apple salad 

THIS IS AN EASY SALAD to toss together, and since carrots and apples have a long shelf life, you probably have some lying around. Get them out of the fruit and vegetable bin and working through your colon.

• • •

Quarter and core 2 apples and grate them on a box grater until you get to the peel. Discard the peel and sprinkle the apple with fresh lemon juice so it doesn't discolor.

Peel and grate 2 carrots, mix the carrots with the apple, and stir in a few spoonfuls of mayonnaise. Toss in some raisins or dried cranberries if you have some. SERVES **4**

slob smarts Carrots are native to Afghanistan and were brought to the New World by colonists.

The day is coming when a single carrot, freshly observed, will set off a revolution.

—PAUL CÉZANNE

caesar salad

WARNING: When you eat this salad, you will become a human crop sprayer of pungent garlic essence. You can practically see the garlic vapors emanating from the salad bowl. On the plus side, if you make this salad correctly, it will surpass your expectations of what a Caesar salad should taste like. Your friends and family will ask you to make it for them often, and you will be known as the Caesar salad expert.

FOR THE CROUTONS

A few slices of Italian bread
Olive oil

FOR THE DRESSING

4 garlic cloves, chopped
4 anchovy fillets
Juice of ½ lemon
Dash of Worcestershire sauce
½ teaspoon Dijon mustard
1 egg yolk
⅓ cup olive oil
Salt and pepper to taste

FOR THE SALAD

2 heads of romaine lettuce, torn into bite-size pieces
½ cup freshly grated Parmesan cheese

To make the croutons: Cut the crusts off the bread slices. Cut the bread into cubes. Toss in a bowl with olive oil to coat. Place the bread cubes on a cookie sheet and toast under the broiler just until browned; stir once or twice as they broil.

To make the dressing: Place the garlic and anchovies in a large wooden salad bowl and mash them into a paste, using a fork. Stir in the lemon juice, Worcestershire sauce, Dijon mustard, and egg yolk.

Whisk in the olive oil, and season with salt and pepper. The dressing should be thick and creamy.

To prepare the salad: Toss the romaine leaves into the salad bowl and add the cheese and croutons. Toss well and serve immediately. SERVES **4**

slob smarts The Caesar salad is attributed to Caesar Cardini, a restaurateur in Tijuana, Mexico. Legend has it that during a hectically busy holiday weekend in 1924 the restaurant's supplies ran short. Mr. Cardini experimented with the ingredients he had on hand and created his namesake salad. He asked the waiters to carry the ingredients to the table and made the salad tableside, declaring, "Give 'em a show." The International Society of Epicures in Paris voted the Caesar salad "the greatest recipe to originate from the Americas in fifty years."

white bean and tuna salad 

A TWIST ON THE PLAIN OLD TUNA SALAD you ate when your mom packed your lunch.

- **1 can white canellini beans, drained and rinsed**
- **1 7-ounce can tuna, drained**
- **2 tablespoons olive oil**
- **1 tablespoon lemon juice**
- **2 tablespoons chopped fresh flat-leaf parsley**

In a medium bowl, combine the beans with the tuna. Toss with the olive oil, lemon juice, and parsley. Serve on toasted white bread or over mixed greens. SERVES **2**

Do not stir up your salad till the mouths are ready for it.

MRS. N. K. M. LEE, *THE COOK'S OWN BOOK*, 1832

fabergé egg salad 

YOU COULD REALLY GILD THE LILY by topping this egg salad with a bit of caviar. I live in the real world, and wind up spooning it on the last heel of white bread left in the bag. Either way, it is a delicious classic, if you can stand the smell.

• • •

Chop up some hard-boiled eggs, and mix with a few spoonfuls of mayonnaise and a bit of Dijon mustard. Season with salt and pepper.

Serve on toast or stuff into hollowed-out cherry or regular tomatoes.

endive, roquefort, and walnut salad 

MY COLLEGE FRIEND LORI and I made this salad when we entertained in our dorm room. It was our first attempt at serving and eating more grown-up fare (even though we served it on a skateboard that rolled out from the kitchen).

• • •

On individual salad plates, arrange spears of Belgian endive leaves in a sunburst pattern. Top with crumbled Roquefort cheese and nuts.

Drizzle with a bit of olive oil and season with salt and pepper.

slob smarts Roquefort cheese is made from ewe's (sheep's) milk, and is one of the world's oldest known cheeses. It was mentioned by Pliny, and was Charlemagne's favorite cheese. In 1411 Charles VI of France gave sole rights to the aging of Roquefort cheese to the village of Roquefort-sur-Soulzon, and even now all Roquefort must be aged in the caves there.

BLT & A salad

THE PHRASE "BRINGING HOME THE BACON" most likely comes from the English custom originating in the twelfth century of giving a young couple bacon if they were still happy after a year of marriage. This is a sandwich deconstructed into a salad—who doesn't love a BLT? The "A" stands for Avocado.

• • •

Tear washed and dried lettuce leaves and toss them in a bowl with chopped avocado and tomato.

Fry some bacon and when it's crisp, tear it into stamp-size pieces and add it to the salad along with the melted fat, for flavor.

Serve immediately, while the bacon is still hot, adding vinaigrette dressing to taste.

slob smarts "A wad of lettuce" is slang for a roll of dollar bills. Pope Sixtus V, a sixteenth-century pontiff, was the son of a gardener. Legend has it that the pope sent a head of lettuce to an old friend in need. When the friend cut it in half, he found that the lettuce head was filled with a stash of paper money. In Italy, if you received a gift of money it was referred to as "one of Sixtus V's salads."

Part of the secret of success in life is to eat what you like and let the food fight it out inside.

—MARK TWAIN

mesclun salad 

with blue cheese, pears, and pecans

THE STRONG FLAVORS of the salty blue cheese, spicy pecans, and sweet pears create a complexity of taste and texture.

Mesclun is a mixture of young leafy greens; it is not a specific type of vegetable. Mescaline is a drug obtained from peyote plants. If you start hallucinating after the first course, you used the wrong kind of vegetation.

- 1 cup pecan halves
- 1 tablespoon butter, melted
- Salt and pepper
- 1 teaspoon chili powder
- 1 14-ounce bag of mesclun salad
- 3 ounces blue cheese, crumbled
- 2 ripe pears, peeled, cored, and cut into matchsticks

Preheat the oven to 350°F.

Toss the nuts with the butter. Season with salt, pepper, and the chili powder and toast the pecans on a cookie sheet for 5 minutes.

Toss the lettuce with dressing. Add the cheese, pecans, and pears and toss again. SERVES **4**

slob smarts Pears have been cultivated for about four thousand years, and are now grown in almost all temperate regions of the world. There are more than five thousand varieties.

spinach salad with bacon and egg 

ONE OF MY FIRST JOBS outside the home was as a salad maker at a French restaurant in New Jersey. For three summers, I slaved under a tyrannical boozy French chef. I learned a lot under his Jack Daniel's dictatorship, and I still rely on the skills he imparted twenty years ago. I must have made a thousand of these salads that summer and I still make them today, a testament to how good the recipe really is.

DRESSING

- 1 tablespoon balsamic vinegar
- 3 tablespoons olive oil
- 1 tablespoon Dijon mustard

SALAD

- 1 pound baby spinach leaves, washed, dried, and stems removed
- 1 red onion, sliced into rings
- 1/4 pound cooked bacon, crumbled into bits
- 4 hard-boiled eggs, quartered
- 6 cherry tomatoes, halved

Whisk the dressing ingredients together in a small bowl or shake in a jar. Toss all the salad ingredients into a large bowl and mix. Pour the dressing over the salad and toss well. SERVES **4**

> Let the salad maker be a spendthrift for oil, a miser for vinegar, a statesman for salt, and a madman for mixing.
>
> —SPANISH PROVERB

subversive salad wedgie 

"ICEBERG LETTUCE," John Waters noted, "is the polyester of vegetables." It is the most popular type of lettuce and is basically devoid of nutritional value. The deeper the color of the lettuce, the more vitamins and nutrients it contains.

1 head iceberg lettuce
1 tomato
Blue cheese dressing or Russian dressing

Slice washed lettuce head into wedges. Quarter the tomato. Arrange on a salad plate, pour dressing over the salad, and serve. SERVES **4**

slob smarts Helping Hands is a nonprofit organization dedicated to improving the quality of life for quadriplegic individuals by training capuchin monkeys to assist them with daily activities. They are a great organization; to find out more, visit www.helpinghands.org.

It's so beautifully arranged on the plate—you know someone's fingers have been all over it.

—JULIA CHILD

basic salad dressings

THE STANDARD PROPORTIONS of oil and vinegar is three parts oil to one part vinegar, plus salt and pepper to taste. I use a jar with a lid to make salad dressing and I marked a line for the correct measurement of oil and vinegar on the outside of the jar using Revlon's Vixen nail polish. Now my husband can make the dressing without asking me twenty questions. I keep any extra dressing in the jar in the refrigerator and use the vinaigrette on salads, as a marinade for raw vegetables, and tossed with leftover cooked vegetables.

Fill the ingredients to the appropriate lines and add seasonings such as herbs, mustard, blue cheese, or citrus juice. Screw on the top, shake, and pour.

all-purpose lemon vinaigrette 

Great with raw vegetables or over avocado slices.

- 1 cup olive oil
- 2/3 cup fresh lemon juice
- 2 tablespoons Dijon mustard
- Salt and pepper to taste

In a small jar, combine all ingredients. Shake well. Refrigerate leftover dressing. MAKES A SCANT CUP

blue cheese dressing 

- 4 ounces blue cheese
- ½ cup vegetable oil
- 1 tablespoon fresh lemon juice
- 1 tablespoon vinegar
- 1 tablespoon Worcestershire sauce

Mash the cheese with a few tablespoons of the oil. Add the remaining oil, the lemon juice, vinegar, and Worcestershire sauce. Beat thoroughly. Store covered in the refrigerator and let warm to room temperature before serving. MAKES ABOUT 1 CUP

slob smarts Don't add dressing to the salad greens too early. Pour it on and toss it just before serving. If you prematurely drench the salad, the leaves will wilt and get more tired-looking than Jerry Lewis after the Labor Day telethon.

dijon vinaigrette 

- ¼ cup red wine vinegar
- 1 teaspoon Dijon mustard
- ¾ cup olive oil
- Salt and pepper to taste

Measure the vinegar and mustard into a small jar. Whisk in the oil. Season with salt and pepper. MAKES 1 CUP

slob smarts Don't be put off by the idea of using your hands to mix food. When tossing salads, you can feel if you need more dressing.

slob smarts Olive oil was so vital and valuable to Mediterranean civilizations that olive oil was awarded to winners of the pre-Olympic games, along with olive wreaths. The second prize was a goat, and third was a woman.

Everything I am,
I owe to spaghetti.

—SOPHIA LOREN

wet noodles

saucy pasta

dishes in

an instant

ACCORDING TO the American Pasta Report, 77 percent of the subjects surveyed stated that they eat pasta at least once a week. The most popular pasta dishes are spaghetti, lasagna, macaroni and cheese, and linguine. **Pasta in the cupboard is like money in the bank.** It is simple to prepare, and many of the sauces in this section are mixed right in the serving bowl, then tossed with the hot pasta noodles. **I return to these recipes like a magnet.** Leonardo da Vinci said, "Simplicity is the ultimate sophistication." That smart Italian could be referring to these deliciously simple pasta dishes.

SLOB SMARTS

The first industrial pasta factory was built in the United States in Brooklyn in 1848. It was built by a French man, and he spread the spaghetti on the roof of the factory to dry in the sun.

Thomas Jefferson is credited with introducing pasta to the United States after sampling it in Naples in the late eighteenth century.

TIPS FOR COOKING PASTA

- Use plenty of water and plenty of salt—2 tablespoons of salt for every gallon of water.
- Bring the salted water to a boil, add the pasta, and bring to a second full boil.
- Fresh pasta cooks in the time it takes to reach the second boil; don't overcook it. Dried pasta will take longer, depending on the thickness and shape.
- Eight ounces of uncooked pasta equal 4 cups of cooked pasta.
- Never rinse pasta after cooking unless specified in a recipe. Just drain in a sturdy colander and toss with a little oil if not using right away.
- Always reserve about half a cup of cooking water. If your sauce is too thick, you can use the reserved water to thin it out.
- When pairing pasta with sauces, the chunkier the shape of the pasta, the heavier the sauce should be.
- If you are using tinned tomato paste (the thick stuff in small cans), a little goes a long way. If you have extra, scoop it out of the can, wrap it in plastic food wrap, and store it in the refrigerator or freezer. You will probably forget about it and end up chucking it. But if you remember, aren't you thrifty?

pasta with
walnut gorgonzola sauce

CHRISTOPHER MORLEY SAID, "No man is lonely eating spaghetti. It requires too much attention." For this dish there is no such thing as too much garlic and cheese; try serving it on a plate that's been warmed in the oven.

1 pound spaghetti or fettuccine
2 garlic cloves, minced
1 tablespoon olive oil
2/3 cup walnut pieces
4 ounces Gorgonzola cheese, crumbled

Bring a large pot of salted water to a boil. Add the pasta and cook just until al dente.

Meanwhile, in a skillet, sauté the garlic in the olive oil over medium heat for 1 minute. Then add the walnut pieces and cook over medium heat for 2 minutes.

When the pasta is cooked, drain it, reserving 1/4 to 1/2 cup of the pasta cooking water. Toss the garlic and walnuts with the hot pasta, then add the Gorgonzola cheese with a few tablespoons of the cooking water. Toss and add a bit more water if needed to make a creamy sauce. SERVES **4**

slob smarts The website www.PastaShoppe.com is a resource for unusually shaped pasta—for example, flamingos, palm trees, snowmen, taxicabs, the star of David, apples, gingerbread men, leaves, footballs and helmets, cats and dogs, and moose. I told my friend Aida Turturro about this, and she said her grandma would roll over in her grave.

penne with black olives and pancetta 

THERE IS NO WAY you can screw this one up.

- 1 pound penne
- 1 pound pancetta (Italian unsmoked bacon) or lean bacon
- ½ teaspoon crushed red pepper flakes
- 3 tablespoons chopped fresh rosemary
- 1 cup black kalamata olives, pitted
- ¼ cup bottled marinara sauce

Bring a large pot of salted water to a boil. Add the pasta and cook just until al dente. Drain.

While the pasta cooks, cut the pancetta into ½-inch dice. In a skillet, cook over medium-high heat until crisp. Drain the fat from the skillet and add the crushed red pepper flakes and rosemary. Cook together for a minute, then stir in the olives.

Toss with the cooked penne and add the marinara sauce. SERVES **4**

slob smarts There are more than five hundred different pasta shapes in Italy, most of which sound more appetizing in their native tongue. Some of the names translated into English are worms, spindles, hats, twins, tubes, thimbles, little boys, little ears, quill pens, and priest stranglers.

The trouble with eating Italian food is that five or six days later you are hungry again.

—GEORGE MILLER

pine nut pasta

TOAST THE PINE NUTS in butter and it will taste as if you actually put an ounce of thought into this dish—but we know that you didn't and it couldn't be easier.

- 1 pound fettucine
- 6 tablespoons butter
- 1 cup pine (pignoli) nuts
- Crushed red pepper flakes to taste

Bring a large pot of salted water to a boil. Add the pasta and cook according to package directions; drain. While the pasta cooks, melt the butter in a frying pan, add the pine nuts, and simmer until golden, about 3 minutes. Season with the pepper flakes. Toss with the hot pasta and serve. SERVES **4**

tomato and basil pasta 

THE UNION OF FRESH PRODUCE and prepared pesto is a lovely thing to behold.

- 1 pound spaghetti or linguine
- 3 large ripe tomatoes, chopped
- ½ cup prepared pesto
- 1 garlic clove, minced
- ¼ cup freshly grated Parmesan cheese

Cook the pasta in a large pot of boiling salted water. Drain.

In a serving bowl, stir together the tomatoes, pesto, and garlic. Add the hot pasta and toss well. Serve with the grated cheese. SERVES **4**

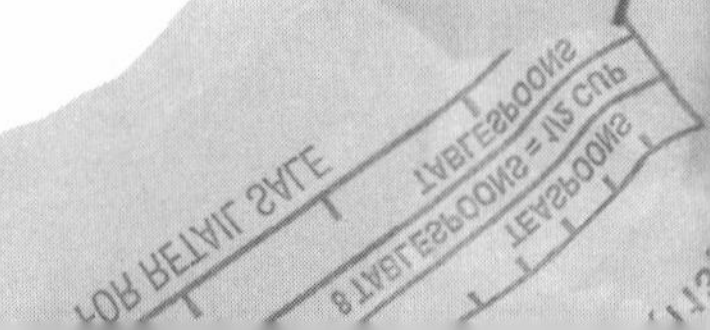

spaghetti with garlic and oil 

THIS RECIPE IS SIMPLE and has enough garlic to make the French seem fragrant. In fact, the garlic aroma may take human form and chase you around the kitchen.

- **1 pound spaghetti**
- **⅓ cup olive oil**
- **8 garlic cloves, minced**
- **Salt and pepper**
- **Freshly grated Parmesan cheese (optional)**

Cook the spaghetti in an abundant amount of salted water as directed on the box.

Meanwhile, in a skillet, heat the oil over medium heat and add the garlic. Cook until the garlic is golden and begins to sizzle. Remove the pan from the heat.

When the pasta is cooked through, drain it and add it to the skillet with the garlic oil. Toss well. Season with salt and pepper. If you feel like it, top with grated Parmesan cheese. SERVES **4**

slob smarts Cooking is like exercise: the less you do it, the less you want to; and the more you do it, the more you want to.

No cook who has attained mastery over her craft ever apologizes for the presence of garlic in her production.

—RUTH GOTTFRIED, THE QUESTING COOK, 1927

saccadatto red sauce 

NICK SACCADATTO, one of the most charming men in the world, has been my barber for years. At his shop he has combined his two passions, cutting hair and Italian food.

In the glass display case where most barbers have brushes, aftershave, dandruff aids, and combs swimming in blue Barbicide, Nick sells Italian specialty foods. There are cans of imported tomatoes and olives, antipasti in jars, dried pasta, and olive oil. In the back, by the sinks where the ladies in the neighborhood get their hair tinted blue, he keeps a crockpot of simmering marinara. As he buzzes and snips his way around my head, he dispenses cooking advice and delicious simple recipes.

Customers come by to get a trim and to pick up ingredients for dinner. The espresso machine hisses all day. The barbershop is a hive of activity. This is Nick's wife Rose's recipe. Use a stainless-steel or enameled cast-iron pot, such as one by Le Creuset.

3 tablespoons olive oil
2 garlic cloves, chopped
1 28-ounce can of peeled Italian plum tomatoes
Salt and pepper to taste
Fresh basil leaves

In a nonreactive pot, heat the olive oil. Add the garlic and sauté, stirring frequently, until golden brown, about 3 minutes. Add the tomatoes and their juices. Season with salt and pepper. Increase the heat to high, bring the sauce to a boil, and cook until the sauce has reduced slightly, about 5 minutes. Reduce the heat to medium low and simmer for 30 minutes. Add a few torn fresh basil leaves just before it's done. MAKES ABOUT **3½** CUPS

spaghetti with carbonara sauce 

CARBONE MEANS "COAL" in Italian, but in this dish it refers to the sprinkling of black pepper, which is meant to look like coal dust. Essentially this recipe is bacon, egg, and cheese on pasta. You have a problem with that?

- **4 bacon strips, chopped**
- **1 pound spaghetti**
- **2 egg yolks**
- **½ cup freshly grated Parmesan cheese**
- **Salt and pepper**

In a skillet, cook the bacon over medium-high heat until crisp. Turn off the heat, and set aside the skillet with bacon.

Bring a large pot of salted water to a boil. Cook the spaghetti according to package instructions, just until al dente.

In a serving bowl, beat the egg yolks with a fork. Slowly pour the bacon and hot bacon fat into the egg yolks, whisking constantly until the yolks are creamy. (Add the bacon fat slowly to avoid cooking the yolks.) Toss the sauce with the hot cooked pasta and grated Parmesan cheese. Season with salt and pepper and serve it as quickly as you can get it on the table. SERVES **4**

I drive way too fast to worry about cholesterol.

—STEVEN WRIGHT

puttanesca pasta

Puttana is the Italian word for a woman of easy virtue. This sauce is quick, easy, and spicy—all virtues in my book.

- 2 28-ounce cans of peeled Italian plum tomatoes
- 1 pound spaghetti
- 1/4 cup olive oil
- 8 garlic cloves, minced
- 1/2 cup kalamata olives, pitted
- 1/4 cup capers, drained
- 1/2 teaspoon dried oregano
- Pinch of crushed red pepper flakes
- 4 anchovy fillets, chopped (optional)

Drain the tomatoes in a colander, and cut into quarters. Bring a large pot of salted water to a boil. Add the pasta and cook according to package directions.

In a large skillet, heat the olive oil over medium-high heat and add the tomatoes and garlic. Stir well, and add the olives, capers, oregano, red pepper flakes, and anchovies, if using. Reduce the heat to medium and cook for 5 minutes, so the flavors get well acquainted.

When the pasta is cooked, drain it, divide it among heated plates, and top it with puttanesca sauce. SERVES **4**

slob smarts Freeze sauces in plastic food storage bags. You can stack them in the freezer to save storage space, then reheat by immersing the bags in hot water.

Life is a combination of love and pasta.

—FEDERICO FELLINI

pesto sauce

PESTO IS A TRINITY of fresh basil, garlic, and olive oil with the addition of cheese and nuts. It doesn't have to be the traditional pine nuts; I mix it up and have used pecans and macadamia nuts with great results. You can make this in the blender, but mashing it all together using a mortar and pestle is more fun and better exercise.

Toss this pesto with pasta or serve as a sauce with vegetables, chicken, or fish. It's also amazing spread on toasted Italian bread.

- **6 garlic cloves, chopped**
- **1/3 cup pine nuts (pignoli)**
- **2 cups lightly packed fresh basil leaves**
- **3/4 cup freshly grated Parmesan cheese**
- **1/2 cup olive oil**

If you are using a mortar and pestle, begin by pounding the garlic, then the nuts. I roughly chop the basil leaves, then pound them with the garlic and nuts. Then I stir in the cheese and oil, a little bit at a time, and mix well. If you prefer to use the blender, put all the ingredients into the container and blend to make a sauce.

MAKES **3 1/2** CUPS

The most indispensable
ingredient of all good home
cooking: love for those
you are cooking for!

—SOPHIA LOREN

john zaccaro jr.'s
penne with vodka sauce

MY FRIEND JOHN ZACCARO founded the world-famous Ravioli Store in New York City. He is the best home cook I know, and this is his easiest—and my favorite—recipe.

- 1 pound penne
- 1/4 teaspoon crushed red pepper flakes, or more to taste
- 1/2 cup vodka
- 4 tablespoons butter
- 1 red onion, sliced
- 2 tablespoons tomato paste
- 3/4 cup heavy cream
- 3/4 cup freshly grated Parmesan cheese
- Salt and pepper to taste

Bring a large pot of salted water to a boil. Add the pasta and cook just until al dente. Drain.

In a cup, steep the red pepper flakes in the vodka and set aside while you get on with making the sauce.

In a skillet, melt the butter, and sauté the onion over medium-high heat until golden and translucent, 5 to 8 minutes. Add the vodka and pepper flakes, and simmer for 2 minutes.

Stir in the tomato paste. Reduce the heat to low and add the cream and grated cheese. Stir well and heat thoroughly. Toss with the drained, cooked pasta. Season with salt and pepper. SERVES **4**

john lilly's tricky rice 

John Lilly is a world-class wisenheimer, my husband's best friend, and a great cook. What I love about John is that he is crunchy on the outside, soft on the inside, just like his recipe for Tricky Rice.

We are lucky to have him visit us up at the farm; he always pitches in and makes a great meal. Even the simple dishes are sublime. He takes an extra step that elevates the everyday dish to something extraordinary. Here is his Tricky Rice recipe.

• • •

Cook the rice in a saucepan, using chicken stock instead of water, and carry on according to package directions.

In a small frying pan, sauté a small sliced onion in olive oil until tender. Toss in a few chopped cloves of garlic, and let them sizzle until golden. When the rice is cooked, fluff it with a fork and stir in the onions and garlic.

The trick here is that the onions and garlic will smell so good as you are cooking, you will trick your guests into thinking that you are doing something special.

slob smarts Throwing rice at newlyweds became popular in the late 1800s. Symbolizing fertility and abundance, the custom has its roots in ancient China.

kitsch-en classics

one-dish wonders you can get on

the table before you can say

"ironic retro hipster"

My aim is simplicity and economy in dressing and preparing foods. If a recipe cannot be written on the face of a three-by-five card, off with its head.

—HELEN NEARING, *SIMPLE FOOD FOR THE GOOD LIFE*, 1980

IF YOU added up all the meals you will prepare in your lifetime (with an average life span of 79 years) you will serve more than 86,000 meals! This is a stupefying number, and when you recognize the enormity of the challenge, **I encourage you to get out of your cooking rut** and take a crack at the recipes in this chapter. Over the years I have invented, experimented with, and re-jiggered this repertoire. It has developed into a collection of basic, reliable meals I can prepare with a minimum of trauma. **Some of these recipes are pure inspiration,** some are adaptations, and every one will put a smile on the mugs of your friends and family.

SLOB SMARTS

It's often said that the kitchen is the most dangerous room in the house. Kitchen accidents can be prevented if you follow these kitchen safety rules.

- **Don't wear long, loose-flowing garments or scarves when cooking; save your Stevie Nicks wardrobe for your host duties.**
- **Always use a step stool or a ladder to reach high cabinets; never stand on a chair or a counter.**
- **Make sure there is enough clearance between the curtains and the stove.**
- **Turn pot handles away from the front of the stove and always use pot holders to remove pots from the stove or oven.**
- **Use salt or baking soda to extinguish small kitchen fires; don't douse them with water.**
- **Keep a fire extinguisher in the kitchen and make sure you and family members know how to use it.**
- **Install a smoke alarm.**
- **Unplug all appliances, especially irons and food processors, immediately after use.**
- **Keep knives sharp and cut away from your body. Always use a cutting board.**
- **Store sharp knives in a separate rack; don't mix them with other kitchen utensils.**
- **Check pilot lights periodically and make sure gas appliances are properly installed and vented and in good working order.**
- **Store all cleaning materials and poisonous materials in a cabinet with a childproof lock.**

cap'n crunch chili

WHEN MY HUSBAND WAS IN COLLEGE he won a chili cook-off. He whipped up the following recipe, which uses Cap'n Crunch cereal scattered on top like croutons.

It is a simple, basic recipe. I make chili every week or so, and I tend to improvise with what is on hand. Instead of diced tomatoes, I've used canned tomato soup or vegetable juice. In place of ground beef, I may add cubes of steak. I'll toss in crumbled, dried, searingly hot peppers, or a pinch of cinnamon and a dash of nutmeg. This recipe is hard to screw up.

- 1 pound ground beef
- 1 big onion, chopped
- 1 garlic clove, minced (optional)
- 2 tablespoons chili powder
- 2 16-ounce cans kidney beans
- 2 16-ounce cans diced tomatoes
- Cap'n Crunch cereal, for garnish

In a large skillet or stockpot, brown the ground beef and onion until the beef is done and the onion is transparent, about 10 minutes. (If you like garlic, add the minced garlic here, too.)

Stir in the chili powder. Add the beans and tomatoes, and let them simmer for about 20 minutes.

Sprinkle with Cap'n Crunch cereal and serve. SERVES **6** TO **8**

Wish I had time for just one more bowl of chili.

—ALLEGEDLY THE LAST WORDS OF KIT CARSON

classic cheese fondue 

THE SWISS TRADITION of "fondue hazing" demands that a woman who drops a piece of bread in the pot plant a kiss on the fella next to her. If a fella fumbles the fondue he has to drain his glass.

Serve fondue with small plates and lots of napkins; it is a messy business.

1 garlic clove, halved
½ cup dry white wine
½ pound (2 cups) grated Emmentaler cheese
½ pound (2 cups) grated Gruyère cheese
1 teaspoon cornstarch
2 teaspoons kirsch
2 loaves French bread, cubed

Rub the inside of a heavy saucepan with the cut side of the garlic, then discard the garlic. Add the wine to the pan and bring to a simmer.

Gradually add the cheeses to the pan, stirring until all the cheese is melted and creamy. Do not boil.

In a small bowl, combine the cornstarch and kirsch, then add to the cheese mixture. Stir to combine well. Transfer to a fondue pot and serve with the French bread. SERVES **4** TO **6**

slob smarts Fondue sets can be found on the cheap at tag sales, but if you still don't have one, serve the fondue in the saucepan you made it in, set over a warming tray.

macaroni and cheese 

THE SUBTLE ALCHEMY of the cheese and macaroni creates a perfect yet easy dish. A generous sprinkling of buttery bread crumbs makes it even better. I've made countless attempts at more complicated recipes, but this one is a cinch to make, and it tastes just as good. I usually monkey around with the seasonings and add a pinch of cayenne pepper and a dash of nutmeg right when I whisk in the flour. Try dry mustard or cumin or mix up the cheese combinations; use what you have on hand. Sometimes I'll chop up bits of prosciutto and toss in some fresh basil. This is a rough-and-ready, slapdash recipe.

1 pound elbow macaroni
8 tablespoons (1 stick) butter, plus more for the dish
¼ cup flour
2 cups milk
2 cups shredded extra-sharp Cheddar cheese
½ cup fresh bread crumbs

Bring a big pot of salted water to a boil and add the macaroni; cook according to the package directions, or just until tender. Drain well and set the macaroni aside.

Preheat the oven to 350°F. Butter a 9 × 9-inch baking dish.

Melt 4 tablespoons of the butter in the same pot. Turn off the heat and whisk in the flour until smooth. Return the pot to the heat and whisk in the milk. Cook for a minute or two, until the sauce thickens. Add the cheese and stir until melted.

Mix in the drained macaroni and pour into the buttered baking dish. Sprinkle with the bread crumbs, dot with the remaining 4 tablespoons of butter, and bake for 20 minutes, or until browned and bubbly. SERVES **6** TO **8**

frito pie

IF YOU ARE WHAT YOU EAT, then I am fast, cheap, and easy.

In 1600, Thomas Moffett wrote, "Men dig their graves with their own teeth and die more by those fatal instruments than the weapons of their enemies." Well, dig in.

- 1 16-ounce bag corn chips
- 1 medium onion, chopped
- 1 cup shredded Cheddar cheese
- 2 15-ounce cans chili

Preheat the oven to 350°F. Sprinkle 2 cups of the corn chips in a 2-quart baking dish. Sprinkle the onion and half of the cheese on top of the chips. Cover with the chili. Top with the remaining corn chips and cheese.

Bake for 20 to 25 minutes, until the dish is heated through and the cheese is melted. SERVES **4** TO **6**

You can tell how long a couple has been married by whether they are on their first, second, or third bottle of Tabasco.

—BRUCE R. BYE

roquefort soufflé

THE WORD *soufflér* means "to blow" in French, and *soufflé* means "blown" or "puffed." A traditional soufflé starts with a thick cooked sauce into which you carefully fold firmly beaten egg whites that inflate with air as they cook. Making a soufflé is not complicated, but it can be intimidating, so I was a bit suspicious when I came across this recipe in a book titled *The Six Minute Soufflé* in which the author claimed to have made a successful soufflé batter in a blender. I tried it and was thrilled with the results. I now keep cheese, eggs, and cream on hand and make this recipe quite often.

This recipe adapts to any kind of cheese. Just keep the key ingredients and experiment with your favorite cheeses and flavorings. The cream cheese gives it the body it needs to rise as it bakes.

- 1 tablespoon butter for greasing the soufflé dish
- 6 eggs
- ½ cup heavy cream
- 1 teaspoon Worcestershire sauce
- Dash of Tabasco sauce
- ¼ teaspoon freshly ground black pepper
- 2 ounces Roquefort cheese, crumbled
- 11 ounces cream cheese, cut into small pieces and softened

Preheat the oven to 350°F. Butter a 6-cup soufflé dish.

In a blender, combine the eggs, cream, Worcestershire sauce, Tabasco, and pepper. Blend until smooth. Add the Roquefort and cream cheese and blend just until mixed.

Pour the batter into the buttered soufflé dish. Set the dish inside a larger pan of warm water, and bake for 40 to 45 minutes for a soft center or 50 to 55 minutes for a firm soufflé. SERVES **6**

slob smarts To serve a soufflé, use two large spoons to scoop out portions.

spinach quiche

IF THE MERE MENTION OF SPINACH QUICHE triggers a Proustian flashback to white wine from jugs and platform shoes, you were probably buzzed for most of the 1970s—and you may not remember that quiche is better than its retro reputation. This is another recipe that you can monkey with: Try a ham-and-cheese version and skip the spinach or add some crumbled bacon. It is like making an omelet in a pastry shell in the oven. It's a gastronomic canvas; make this recipe your own work of art.

8 ounces Swiss cheese, shredded
1 unbaked pie shell
1 10-ounce box frozen spinach, thawed and drained
1 onion, finely chopped
3 eggs
1 cup milk
Pinch of cayenne pepper
Salt and pepper to taste
Pinch of nutmeg

slob smarts

Quiche can also be made without pastry crust. Butter a pie plate with 3 tablespoons of butter and then press 1 cup of toasted bread crumbs into the butter.

Preheat the oven to 350°F.

Sprinkle about half of the cheese over the bottom of the pie shell, then layer the spinach and onion over the cheese.

In a mixing bowl, beat together the eggs, milk, cayenne, salt, pepper, and nutmeg and pour into the shell.

Sprinkle on the remaining cheese and bake for 45 minutes, or until the quiche is set in the center. SERVES **6**

I asked the barmaid for a quickie. The man next to me said, "It's pronounced quiche." —LUIGI AMADUZZI

luciano pavarotti's
corn-dog necklace 

I ADORE MR. PAVAROTTI and I couldn't believe my luck when I was asked to be a guest on the *Tonight Show* the same evening that Mr. Pavarotti was scheduled to perform. In appreciation of his lavish talent that he has shared with the world, I wanted to make him a gift. My friends Sidney and Billy Bob assisted me and we decided to make Mr. Pavarotti a corn-dog necklace.

We went to the grocery store and bought a few boxes of frozen corn dogs (hot dogs dipped in corn bread, impaled on a stick, and deep-fried; kind of like a pork-sicle).

The boys drilled holes through the wooden sticks and we laced the corn dogs on a cord to make a necklace. Our thought was that if Mr. Pavarotti got hungry he could wear his necklace on stage and take a few bites. This would free him to keep his mind on the music and not on lunch.

We left the necklace for him in his dressing room. We even provided a pocket protector so he could keep condiments in his left breast pocket. Although he never thanked us for the gift, I like to think that he enjoyed it.

One of the very nicest things about life is the way we must regularly stop whatever it is we are doing and devote our attention to eating.

—LUCIANO PAVAROTTI

afternoon tea

AN INFORMAL tea served at the table or on a tray in the living room is a rewarding way to punctuate the afternoon. Laurie Colwin, the late writer whom I regard with admiration, encouraged her readers to serve afternoon tea for children's parties. Most people get hungry around four or five o'clock, and small crustless sandwiches, jam with bread, stuffed deviled eggs, and a small cake and plate of sweets is a great lineup. For something a bit different, you could toast sandwiches on a waffle iron. If unexpected hordes of children darken your doorway, have them make their own Peanut Butter and Jelly Sushi (page 92), a form of tea sandwich of which I think Ms. Colwin would have approved.

And note that for every ten minutes that you are late picking up your child from a friend's birthday party, you shorten your friendship with his or her parents by one year.

There are few hours in life more agreeable than the hour dedicated to the ceremony known as afternoon tea.

—HENRY JAMES, *THE PORTRAIT OF A LADY*, 1881

peanut butter and jelly sushi 

WHEN WE WERE KIDS, my mom once held a meeting in our dining room with the neighborhood ladies to plan the annual Fourth of July block-party celebration. While they sat in the dining room, my sister Kate and I were working on a project at the kitchen table, where we could eavesdrop. They were discussing the menu when we heard the resident crone, Mrs. F., say, "Don't bother making steaks for the children; we can just throw jelly sandwiches at them."

Kate and I howled with indignation, although the image of getting pelted with jelly sandwiches by a vicious old goat was oddly compelling. Later that evening my sisters and I returned the sentiment and toilet-papered her house.

To this day, when I ask Kate what she is going to make for dinner, she will reply, "Oh, I'm just going to throw jelly sandwiches at the kids."

Note: As I was writing this recollection, I called Kate to do some fact-checking. She insisted that I mention that Mrs. F. had two little fluffy white dogs. Mrs. F. didn't like that her dogs barked and had the dogs' voice boxes removed. This may be neighborhood kid folklore, but Kate wanted me to pass it on.

• • •

Cut the crust off a slice of soft white bread and roll the bread with a rolling pin to flatten it.

Spread peanut butter and jelly or marshmallow creme on the bread. Roll it up and press chocolate sprinkles into the squishy bread. Slice into pieces the size of California sushi rolls. EACH ROLL MAKES **3** PIECES

slob smarts Food historians note that peanut butter was invented in the 1890s, but there is no note of peanut butter and jelly sandwiches until the 1940s, when both were a part of the U.S. military's meal rations during World War II.

piglets in a blanket 

THESE SNACKS are so good that people have been known to make pigs out of themselves when they come out of the oven.

- **1 can refrigerated crescent rolls**
- **8 small cocktail franks**
- **Dijon mustard**
- **16 peppercorns and a few pieces of uncooked fusilli pasta broken into pigtail-sized pieces, for decoration**

Preheat the oven to 400°F.

Unroll the dough and separate it into triangular sections. Spread each section with mustard, then wrap each section around a cocktail frank, starting from the wide end.

Place each piglet on a baking sheet and press two peppercorns into the franks to make the piglet's eyes. Add a piece of fusilli for the tail.

Bake the piglets for 10 to 12 minutes, until golden. MAKES **8** PIGLETS

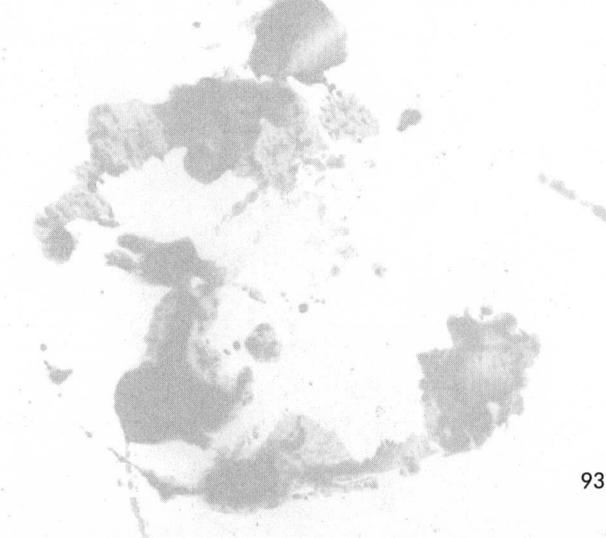

sunday night lasagna

SUNDAY EVENING has its own brand of misery. The glorious liberty of the weekend is tainted by the looming school week ahead. When we were kids, the Sunday night TV program *60 Minutes* tormented me and my siblings. The exaggerated sound effect of that stopwatch—*tick, tick, tick, tick*—still gets my stomach in a knot. We would make up words to the ticking clock: "Tick-tick-tick-tick, you didn't finish your homework"; "Tick tick tick tick, Sister Ginetta is teaching tomorrow." To console us, our mother would make Sunday Night Lasagna.

CHEESE FILLING

16 ounces ricotta cheese
2 eggs
1 teaspoon dried oregano
Salt and pepper to taste

LASAGNA

4 cups Saccadatto Red Sauce (see page 74)
1 8-ounce package lasagna noodles, cooked or no-boil type
1 pound baby spinach leaves with stems, rinsed
1 pound (4 cups) shredded mozzarella cheese

To make the filling, in a large bowl mix together the ricotta cheese, eggs, oregano, salt, and pepper.

To assemble the lasagna, in a 9 × 13-inch baking dish spread a thin layer of the tomato sauce. Arrange a layer of lasagna noodles, and spread about one-third of the ricotta mixture on top of the noodles. Spread about one-third of the spinach leaves and one-third of the shredded cheese, and top with a layer of sauce. Repeat this process, creating two more layers. Top with another layer of sauce and shredded cheese.

Preheat the oven to 400°F. Cover the dish with foil and bake for 30 minutes. Remove the foil and bake for another 15 minutes, or until the cheese is lightly browned. SERVES **8** TO **12**

slob smarts Food preferences and family mealtime routines are among our most ingrained behaviors. It has been noted that immigrants will abandon the language of their homeland before they abandon the food choices and meal patterns with which they were raised.

garlicky parmesan bread 

THIS JAZZED UP garlic bread is a perfect complement to Sunday Night Lasagna. It's a few more extra steps than plain old ordinary garlic bread, but then who deserves the effort more than your family?

½ cup mayonnaise
½ cup Parmesan cheese, shredded
3 cloves of garlic, minced, or more to taste
1 loaf of Italian bread, sliced

Preheat broiler.

Mix together the mayonnaise, Parmesan cheese, and garlic. Spread on bread slices. Place slices on a baking sheet and broil until golden brown. SERVES **6** TO **8**

cheat a pizza

THE CRUST IS THE MOST CRUCIAL PART of any pie, so why reinvent the wheel every time you want to serve delicious hot pizza in your home? My suggestion is to go to your local pizzeria and purchase some pizza dough.

TOPPING SUGGESTIONS

Artichoke hearts and fontina cheese

Prosciutto and shredded mozzarella

Pesto and goat cheese

Roasted red peppers and ricotta cheese

When you feel like cheatin' a pizza, turn the oven on to 500°F and let it preheat while you stretch and shape the dough. Sprinkle cornmeal on a baking sheet, and press the dough onto the pan. Top with sauce, cheese, and whichever toppings you prefer (see above). Bake for about 15 minutes, or until the crust is golden brown and the cheese is bubbly. Cut into small squares or slices and serve. MAKES **1** PIZZA

slob smarts Yogi Berra once ordered a pizza and was asked if he wanted it cut into four slices or eight. "Better make it four," he responded. "I don't think I can eat eight." In fact, why cut your pizza into slices? Use a cookie cutter and stamp out shaped pieces.

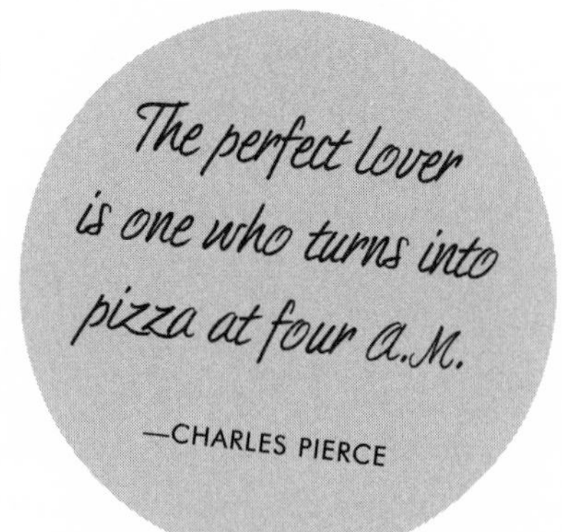

Poultry is for cookery what canvas is for painting.

—JEAN-ANTHELME BRILLAT

tastes like chicken

a peck of

tasty poultry recipes

CHICKEN is a cook's canvas, its versatility its virtue. The average American eats more than 80 pounds of chicken per year, and more than half of all chicken dishes ordered in restaurants are fried chicken. We raise chickens on our farm both for their eggs and for their meat and I serve it often.

One night my husband unexpectedly invited a crowd back to our apartment for dinner. I had about an hour to figure out how to feed eight guests, and **in a moment's desperation I came up with "chicken fight night."** While I roasted a chicken in my countertop Sunbeam rotisserie, John went to Kentucky Fried Chicken, Popeye's, Boston Market, and Church's and bought chicken from each franchise. I made a batch of biscuits, spinach, mashed potatoes, and a salad. We set the various chicken selections on platters buffet style and let our guests vote for the best chicken. My chicken won the chicken fight and

ever since that victory my rotisserie has been my favorite kitchen appliance. Last year I even roasted our Thanksgiving turkey breast in it. It was fantastic and essentially effortless.

grilled chicken

THERE IS NOTHING WORSE than undercooked chicken. It is like poultry-flavored Jell-O. Chicken seems to always take a long time on the grill, and often by the time the interior juices run clear, the outside is charred. To prevent this unsavory situation, you can precook the poultry in the oven until it's about halfway done, then finish it on the grill, cooking it about 6 inches above the heat source. To keep the meat moist, and for best flavor, keep the skin on the chicken while grilling.

Meat on the bone takes longer to cook than boneless cuts. Figure about 20 minutes per pound on the bone—though it will vary depending on the grill temperature. Baste the chicken every 10 minutes or so with an oil-based marinade. Barbecue sauce is high in sugar and fat, which will burn, so if you want to use it, wait to coat the chicken during the last 10 minutes of cooking, and serve some extra sauce on the side.

slob smarts Line the bottom of your oven with strips of foil to collect spills. If you have a gas oven, be careful that you do not cover any vents. Line the inside of the stove burners with aluminum foil.

beer can chicken

GET OUT OF your cooking rut; dinner doesn't have to be a mind-numbing chore. Also known as beer butt chicken, this culinary surprise can be made on the grill or in the oven. The visual of a chicken standing upright on a beer can or your barbecue grill will get a lot of laughs, and it tastes great.

1 5-pound chicken
¼ cup olive oil
¼ cup Duff's Roadkill Helper (see page 157)
1 12-ounce can of beer
4 garlic cloves, peeled and smashed

Rinse the chicken and pat dry. Rub oil all over the chicken skin and inside the cavity. Sprinkle 1 tablespoon of the spice rub into the cavity, and rub the rest all over the chicken.

Open the beer can, drain off a few sips, and toss the smashed garlic into the can. Holding the chicken upright, push the southern end of the chicken over the beer can, so it looks as if the chicken is standing at attention.

To cook in the oven: preheat the oven to 350°F. Place the chicken in a shallow roasting pan or baking dish. Roast until the juices run clear, about 1¼ hours.

To cook on the grill: Stand the chicken upright on a hot grill. Cover the grill with a lid or a large stockpot. Grill until the juices run clear, about 1¼ hours. (Grilling times vary, depending on the size of your chicken and heat of your coals.) SERVES **4** TO **6**

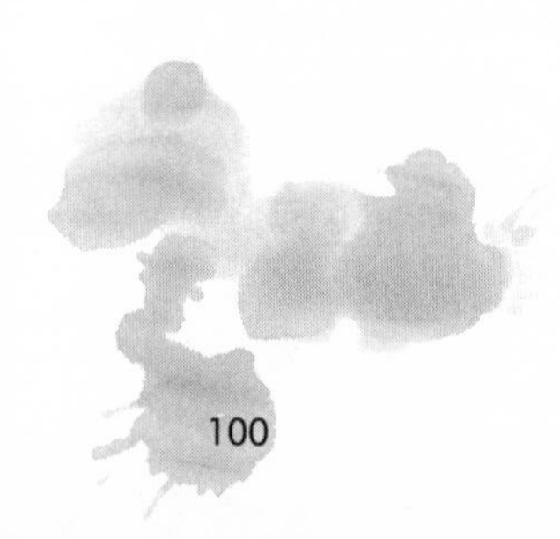

lazybones chicken
in barbecue sauce

THE NAME SAYS IT ALL. This is the recipe I rely on when I have a big group of kids to feed. The most important step is to line your baking dish or roasting pan with foil. One time I forgot and was left with the dirtiest baking pan in the world. I could not get it clean and had to donate it to the Smithsonian Institution. It is now part of an exhibit on slovenly cooks.

3- to 4-pound package of chicken pieces, on the bone
2 cups bottled barbecue sauce

Preheat the oven to 350°F. Line a baking dish or roasting pan with aluminum foil.

Place the chicken pieces in the pan and toss with the barbecue sauce. Cover with another piece of foil and bake for 1 hour.

After 1 hour, remove the top piece of foil, and continue baking for another 10 to 15 minutes, until the chicken is tender. SERVES **4** TO **6**

slob smarts In Gainesville, Georgia—the chicken capital of the world—it is illegal to eat chicken with a fork.

simple roast chicken 

I FIND THAT trusting those pop-up gizmos that are meant to tell you when your chicken is done will pretty much guarantee a dried-out, overcooked chicken. Wouldn't it be great if you could throw a handful of popcorn into the cavity and when you heard the kernels pop you'd know it was done to perfection? Unfortunately, it doesn't work. I know; I tried. Instead, try this simple roast chicken.

• • •

Preheat the oven to 325°F. Stuff a 3-pound chicken with half a lemon.

Baste with juice from the other lemon half mixed with 1/4 cup melted butter.

Bake for about 1 1/2 hours, or until the juices run clear when you prick the thigh with the point of a knife. SERVES **2** TO **4**

VARIATION Throw some garlic cloves, sliced onion, and whole new potatoes into the roasting pan. When the chicken is done the vegetables will be somewhat overdone, but they are good that way.

slob smarts In Chinese culture, a chicken on the table is a symbol of good luck—even though it isn't very lucky for the chicken.

broiled lemon chicken 

RAO'S IS ONE of the most famous and exclusive Italian restaurants in New York City and it's known for its simple but delicious menu. It is more like a club than a restaurant; it is impossible to just walk in or even call for a reservation. Every table every night is booked by regulars, and to dine there you have to be invited by a regular. Whenever I am lucky enough to have an opportunity to dine at Rao's I order the lemon chicken. This recipe is almost as good as theirs.

4 pounds chicken parts
Salt and pepper
1 cup fresh lemon juice, from about 3 lemons
½ cup olive oil
½ cup white wine

Rinse the chicken and pat dry with paper towels. Season the pieces with salt and pepper.

In a medium bowl, whisk together the lemon juice and 1/4 cup of the olive oil. Pour into a resealable plastic bag. Add the chicken, and marinate in the refrigerator for at least 4 hours; overnight is better.

Preheat the broiler. Remove the chicken pieces from the marinade (don't throw the marinade away) and pat them dry with paper towels. Place them on a shallow baking sheet and brush them with the remaining olive oil. Broil until the chicken is golden brown, then turn the pieces over and repeat.

Arrange the broiled chicken in a large skillet and pour the marinade and wine over them. Cover and simmer for 20 minutes, until the meat is tender and cooked through. Serve with the lemon wine sauce. SERVES **4** TO **6**

thai chicken cutlets 

IF MOST OF YOUR CHICKEN DISHES turn out duller than Canadian history, try this spectacularly easy recipe. (Look in the international section of your supermarket for small cans of red, yellow, or green curry paste.)

1 cup canned coconut milk
3 tablespoons Thai curry paste
6 boneless, skinless chicken cutlets

Whisk together the coconut milk and curry paste and pour into a resealable plastic bag.

Add the chicken cutlets and marinate in the refrigerator for 1 hour. Transfer the chicken and marinade to a heavy skillet and cook over high heat until cooked through, turning the chicken as needed. SERVES **6**

slob smarts Turn a metal colander upside down over a skillet when frying to cut down on splatters.

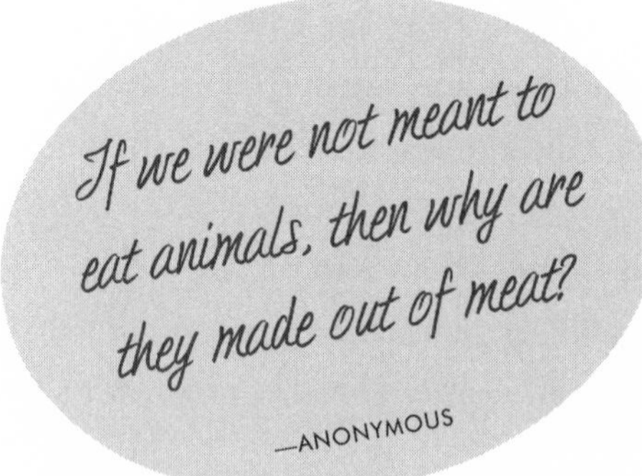

you-slaved-for-minutes
baked chicken and couscous 

BONELESS CHICKEN COOKS in minutes and couscous takes 1 minute to prepare. Still, this dish tastes as if you really put in some effort.

- 2 tablespoons olive oil
- 4 boneless chicken breasts
- 1 cup couscous
- 1½ cups chicken broth
- Salt and pepper
- Juice and zest of 1 lemon
- ½ cup pitted black olives
- Chopped fresh flat-leaf parsley, for garnish

Preheat the oven to 350°F.

In a skillet, heat 1 tablespoon of the olive oil and cook the chicken breasts on each side until golden, about 2 minutes for each side. The chicken will not be cooked through.

Place the couscous in a medium baking dish or casserole. Add the broth, the remaining tablespoon of olive oil, and salt and pepper, and stir. Place the chicken breasts on the couscous. Pour the lemon juice and zest over the chicken breasts. Toss in the olives and cover the dish with aluminum foil

Bake for 25 to 30 minutes, or until the chicken is cooked through. Fluff the couscous with a fork and garnish with the parsley. It will give the dish an earnest quality and make it look as if you tried.

SERVES **4**

The greatest dishes are the simplest dishes.

—ESCOFFIER

"tastes like chicken" stir-fry 

ON MOTT STREET in Manhattan's Chinatown there is a noisy, dark video arcade where for fifty cents you can play tic-tac-toe with a chicken. I have played against him and he almost always wins. That is one tough cock. Unlike this one.

- **1 tablespoon vegetable oil**
- **1 red bell pepper, cored, seeded, and chopped**
- **1 small red onion, diced**
- **1 pound boneless, skinless chicken breast, cut into 1-inch strips**
- **1 cup cashews**
- **3 tablespoons hoisin sauce**

Heat the oil in a nonstick skillet or wok for about a minute over high heat. Add the bell pepper and onion, cook for about a minute, then stir. Cook for another minute. Add the chicken, and let the pieces cook on one side for a minute, then stir. Cook for another minute or so. By now, the vegetables and chicken should be just cooked through.

Lower the heat to medium and stir in the cashews and hoisin sauce. Cook for about 30 seconds, and add a few tablespoons of water to create a thin sauce that covers the chicken and vegetables.
SERVES **4**

slob smarts Speaking of tough cocks, Mike the Headless Wonder Chicken from Fruita, Colorado, was featured in *Life* magazine in 1946 for surviving eighteen months without a head. His owner, Mr. Lloyd Olsen, was butchering Mike for dinner and although he chopped off Mike's head, most of a chicken's reflex actions are controlled by the brain stem, which was left intact. The "Wonder Chicken" gained his owner fame and fortune and holds a Guinness World Record. Each year Mike's spirit is celebrated in Fruita on the third weekend in May.

coconut-lime
chicken shish kebabs

SHISH KEBABS ARE GREAT for entertaining because they can be prepared ahead of time and are easy to grill and serve. The coconut milk and lime-ginger marinade give the chicken a kick. And by the way, if the professor on Gilligan's Island can make a radio out of a coconut, why can't he fix a hole in a boat?

- **1 14-ounce can coconut milk**
- **2 tablespoons peeled and minced fresh ginger**
- **2 tablespoons soy sauce**
- **2 garlic cloves, minced**
- **1 tablespoon honey**
- **Zest and juice of 1 lime**
- **1/4 teaspoon cayenne pepper or dash of Tabasco sauce**
- **2 pounds boneless, skinless chicken breasts, cut into 2-inch chunks**

In a resealable plastic bag, mix together the coconut milk, ginger, soy sauce, garlic, honey, lime zest and juice, and cayenne pepper. Toss in the chicken, and marinate in the refrigerator for an hour or two.

Prepare a grill or preheat the broiler.

Thread the chicken onto skewers.

Cook them on a medium-hot grill or in the broiler for about 5 minutes on each side, turning once. SERVES **4** TO **6**

slob smarts There's a place for imagination and ingenuity in the kitchen, but if you are the first person to poach chicken breasts in clam juice, there probably is a reason for it.

chicken piccata 

MY FRIEND COURTNEY FEBBRORIELLO, author of *Wife of the Chef* and with her husband owner of the wildly successful, award-winning restaurant Metro Bis in Simsbury, Connecticut, wrote that she believes most people eat the same five things over and over. (In fashion circles, there is a similar widely circulated belief that most people wear 20 percent of their wardrobe 80 percent of the time.) In my home, this recipe for Chicken Piccata, adapted from *Cook's Illustrated* magazine, is a winner. I make double batches and keep extra in the freezer. Having a pan of Chicken Piccata in the deep freeze is like finding money on the street. Unless, of course, you forget to cook it.

One night when we were having friends over for dinner, I grabbed a pan of Chicken Piccata from the freezer and popped it in the oven. I had neglected to turn the oven on. When I went to serve the chicken, it was frozen solid.

In a panic, I cranked the oven up to 500°F. in the hope that the chicken would cook more quickly. What a disaster! When I served it, the sauce was boiling hot, but the inside of the cutlets looked like chicken-flavored gelato. Our guests politely ate around the frozen bits, and all the side dishes were devoured.

- 1/4 cup flour
- Salt and pepper
- 4 boneless, skinless chicken breasts, pounded thin
- 3 tablespoons olive oil
- 4 garlic cloves, minced
- 1 cup chicken broth
- Juice and zest of 1 lemon
- 1/4 cup chopped parsley
- 1 tablespoon butter

OPTIONAL

- 1/4 cup capers
- Red pepper flakes to taste
- 1/4 pound chopped prosciutto

In a plastic food storage bag, mix the flour with a few shakes of salt and pepper. One at a time, place the chicken breasts into the flour, and shake to coat lightly.

In a skillet or sauté pan, heat 2 tablespoons of the olive oil over medium-high heat, and cook the chicken breasts for 2 minutes on each side, turning once.

When all the chicken is cooked, place the breasts in a baking dish, cover with foil, and hold in a warm oven—250°F.—while you make the sauce.

In the same pan in which you cooked the chicken, heat the remaining tablespoon of oil, and sauté the garlic for 1 minute over medium-high heat.

Add the chicken broth to the garlic, stir, and add the lemon juice. Stir, and cook for about 5 minutes, until the sauce reduces and the flavors get acquainted.

Reduce the heat to low, and stir in the parsley, butter, and lemon zest (if you want to add capers, red pepper flakes, or chopped prosciutto, do it here). When the butter is melted, and the sauce is enriched, remove from the heat.

Pour the sauce over the chicken and serve over pasta, mashed potatoes, or rice. Garnish with chopped parsley and lemon slices.

If you want to prepare this dish in advance, you can make the sauce a day early. Cook the chicken and hold in a warm oven, covered with foil. Prepare the sauce, and reheat and pour over chicken right before serving.

And don't forget to make sure you turn on the oven. SERVES **4**

fried chicken cutlets 

MUSIC LEGEND BO DIDDLEY is known for his contributions to popular American music and for traveling to his concert dates with an electric chicken fryer. Mr. Diddley would fry up chicken before his gig and share pieces with a few lucky fans.

Boneless, skinless chicken breasts (1 per person)
Milk
Seasoned flour
Cornflake crumbs or cracker crumbs (I've even used smashed up Cap'n Crunch or Rice Krispies)
Vegetable oil, for frying

Slice the chicken breasts into 1-inch-thick strips; dip in milk and then in the seasoned flour (use whatever you like: garlic, paprika, salt, pepper, cayenne pepper). Roll the floured strips in the cornflake crumbs or cracker crumbs.

In a skillet, heat 1½ inches of oil and fry the strips until the juices run clear when you poke them with a fork. Don't crowd the pan.

VARIATION Splash the chicken strips with Worcestershire sauce, then drop in a resealable plastic bag filled with corn-muffin mix. Toss the chicken with the muffin mix to coat and fry until golden and the juices run clear.

slob smarts When breading cutlets, use one hand for wet ingredients and one hand for dry. This way, when the phone rings, and it's George Clooney asking you to marry him, you will have a relatively clean hand with which to answer the phone and say yes.

scrappy cacciatore

CACCIATORE IS ITALIAN for "hunter." The best thing about this simple version of the class chicken cacciatore is that you don't have to exhaust yourself hunting for the ingredients. That, and you don't have to whack and pluck the chicken.

- **3 tablespoons olive oil**
- **4 boneless, skinless chicken breasts**
- **2 cups chunky-style spaghetti sauce with vegetables**
- **1 green pepper, seeded, cored, and cut into strips**
- **1 pound spaghetti**
- **¼ cup freshly grated Parmesan**

In a skillet, heat the olive oil over medium-high heat. Add the chicken breasts and cook until browned, turning once. Add the spaghetti sauce and pepper strips, cover the skillet, and simmer on low for about 20 minutes, or until the chicken is tender and cooked through.

While the chicken cooks, bring a large pot of salted water to a boil. Cook the spaghetti according to package directions and drain well.

Serve the chicken over the pasta and top with the grated Parmesan. SERVES **4**

If the eyes are the window to the soul, could the nostrils be the screen door to the stomach?

white castle stuffing 

A little kid is asked if he liked his Thanksgiving turkey dinner. He replies, "I didn't like the turkey, but I did like the bread he ate."

My dad heard about using White Castle hamburgers as stuffing, and he intends to make it this year for all of us. I was able to pry the recipe out of him. Go to White Castle and buy a bag of burgers. Remove the pickles, tear the burgers and buns in half, and shove the halves in the turkey cavity. Roast as usual.

SCRAPPY THANKSGIVING

Inviting your entire extended family over for Thanksgiving is like committing culinary hara-kari, and the vision of twenty masticating relatives isn't my idea of a holiday. If there's no avoiding it, buy a bunch of lottery tickets and put one at each place setting. Someone might hit the jackpot, and a rich relative is a lot easier to take than any other kind.

If it is a small group and you favor white meat, consider roasting a turkey breast instead of a whole bird. Or try cooking the turkey on your grill; it frees the oven for side dishes.

Chances are your guests will ask if they can bring anything. Tell them, "Yes, an appetizer, a salad, two side dishes, and an eighteen-pound stuffed, roasted turkey." And presto, let the thanksgiving commence.

When you are hosting a big event like Thanksgiving dinner, clear the countertops of the toaster, blender, canisters, and other kitchen accessories and appliances that you are not using that day. Create extra counter space by placing large trays and cookie sheets across pulled-out kitchen drawers, or set up an ironing board.

grilled turkey

THE BARBECUE KETTLE or gas grill will roast a tasty, moist turkey that will keep your oven free to bake the side dishes and desserts. Steven Raichlen, author of *BBQ USA* and a fan of barbecued turkey, inspired this recipe. A standard kettle grill or a 2-burner gas grill will accommodate a 12-pound turkey.

• • •

Lightly oil the exterior of the bird. Season with a dry rub or make your own by combining 1 tablespoon each of salt, pepper, paprika, brown sugar, and lemon zest. Use your imagination; it is hard to screw it up.

Light the coals, and when they are hot, rake them to the sides and place a drip pan in the center.

Place the turkey over the drip pan and cover (you can invert a big stockpot to act as a cover if your grill cover doesn't fit). Grill for 2½ to 3 hours, replenishing the coals every hour by dropping 10 to 15 coals on each side.

The turkey is done when your meat thermometer reads 180°F. in the thigh.

For gas grills, light one side or the front and back of 3 burners. Place the turkey away from the flames. SERVES **6** TO **8**

slob smarts Label the inside of your cupboards and drawers. You need a system for what goes where, and when you have guests helping out they won't nag you to death asking where you keep your serving spoons.

barbecued turkey hash 

If I had to make a Mount Rushmore of my personal heroines, the four heads carved in stone would be Dorothy Parker, Gloria Steinem, Mother Teresa, and Joan Hamburg. You are most likely familiar with the first three, and if you have heard Joan Hamburg's call-in radio show, you know why she is on my list. Listening to her show is like listening to a friend dispensing great advice. She is smart, witty, positive, and a wellspring of good ideas. Here is Joan's foolproof recipe for leftover turkey. After you make this you will join the Joan Hamburg fan club as well.

- **4 medium potatoes, peeled and cut into ½-inch cubes**
- **3 tablespoons olive oil**
- **2 medium onions, coarsely chopped**
- **Salt and pepper**
- **2 to 3 cups diced leftover cooked turkey**
- **1 cup bottled barbecue sauce**

In a saucepan, cover the potatoes with water and boil until tender, about 12 minutes. Don't let them get mushy. Drain well.

In a skillet, heat the oil, add the onions, and cook on medium-high heat until soft, 6 to 8 minutes. Reduce the heat to moderate and cook until brown. Season with salt and pepper and add the potatoes and turkey. Cook until hot.

Stir in the barbecue sauce, heat through, and serve. SERVES **4** TO **6**

Mother Teresa said, "Not all of us can do great things, but we can all do small things with great love." Why not flip to the sweets section and whip up a batch of cookies and deliver them to an old cranky geezer in the neighborhood and make her day.

Red meat is not bad for you. Blue-green meat, now **that** *is bad for you.*

—TOMMY SMOTHERS

chew the fat

carnivorous main courses

The smell of roasting meat together with that of burning fruitwood and dried herbs, as voluptuous as incense in a church, is enough to turn anyone into a budding gastronome.

—CLAUDIA RODEN, *PICNIC*, 1981

where does beef come from?

MY LATE FATHER-IN-LAW was a gentlemen farmer who raised a herd of Belted Galloways, an exotic, boutique beef cattle. He named three cows Almay, Revlon, and Duff, in my honor. My husband has since inherited this family farm and we are continuing the tradition. For most of my life, I would have characterized myself as an indoor type of gal, **so the fact that I spend part of my week living on a farm still comes as a surprise.**

I've learned a lot living on the farm, and I would say the biggest lesson is the beauty and brutality of the life cycle and the food chain. **Our cows are bovine charisma on the hoof** and, yes, we do slaughter and eat them. I am now much more educated about farming practices, and have a deep appreciation and gratitude for small family-owned farms and the people who run them. They work so hard, and provide such a wonderful product, **I felt it was the least I could do to learn how to make a decent roast, steak, or stew.** Any of the recipes in this chapter will honor the animal in question and the folks who raised it—not to mention those who share your table.

If you burn the main course, simply toss in the phrase *"al carbone"* (Italian for "with coal") when presenting the dish, as in, "Tonight, we are having steak *al carbone.*" You can also go the retro route and say you are reviving "blackened" cuisine from the eighties.

If it's really dire, claim you've established your own satellite branch of the Museum of Burnt Food. (For more information on the Museum of Burnt Food go to www.burntfoodmuseum.com/, the site that celebrates the art of culinary disaster.)

SLOB SMARTS

roasting tips

As Joan Crawford's character, Crystal, stated in the film version of Clare Boothe Luce's *The Women,* "If you throw a lamb chop in the oven, what's to keep it from getting done?" Roast meats could not be easier to prepare, especially for a dinner party. The meat fends for itself in the oven while you can focus your attention on more stimulating pursuits, like waxing your mustache or writing your congressman.

Cooking a simple beef roast, leg of lamb, or pork tenderloin takes minimal effort and produces maximal results. A roast makes it look like you tried, and if you can fake earnestness in the kitchen, you are home free in my book.

Roasting is cooking with dry heat. The intent is to create a seared exterior while the interior remains moist and tender. The ideal way to cook a roast is to place it on a rack set inside a roasting pan, so the hot air can circulate around it. The rack will prevent the underside of the roast from stewing and frying in its own rendered fat. If you don't have a roasting rack, you can improvise with a wire cake rack. If you don't have a wire cake rack, make a rack out of hardy vegetables, like carrots, parsnips, turnips, or potatoes and onions, and set your roast on top. The vegetables will overcook, but I like them that way.

Roasts are cooked uncovered. Large chunks of meat that are covered with a layer of fat will stay moist as the fat melts. Leaner meats like chicken and smaller cuts, those weighing less than 4 pounds, are improved if they are basted every half hour or so with the pan drippings so they don't dry out. If you calculate 20 minutes per pound at 350°F., you should produce a successful roast.

cowboy steak

THE CRAZY AMOUNT OF SMOKE generated by this cooking technique will smite the nostrils, and the kitchen will get so smoky, it will look like the van in Cheech and Chong's movie *Up in Smoke.* When the steaks are done, let them rest for a few minutes while you open up the windows and flap some towels around to disperse the smoke. A short resting period will let the juices settle into the meat so they don't run onto the cutting board when you slice the meat.

2 1¼-inch-thick ribeye steaks
½ cup kosher salt

Pat the steaks dry with paper towels.

Sprinkle the salt evenly in the bottom of a cast-iron skillet. Heat the skillet over high heat for about 5 minutes, until the salt begins to crackle and lightly smoke.

Place the steaks in the hot skillet on top of the salt. Cook for 5 minutes, turn the steaks over, and cook the other side for another 5 minutes for medium-rare. Transfer the steaks to a cutting board and let them rest for 5 minutes before slicing. SERVES **2**

SLOB SMARTS

If you cook, things are going to get burned once in a while. With this in mind, I suggest you outfit your kitchen with at least one cast-iron skillet. They can take all kinds of abuse. If you were not lucky enough to inherit one, they can be found at garage sales. New ones, both plain and enamel-coated, are sold at cookware and hardware shops. Cast iron must be seasoned. Rub the cooking surface with vegetable oil and place in a hot oven for 1 hour. The best way to clean cast iron is to rub the skillet with a handful of salt and a bit of lemon. It isn't necessary to wash or submerge in soapy water. If you do, you will have to reseason the skillet. Set wet pans on the stovetop and turn on the heat to evaporate the water so the cast iron will not rust.

steak diane

THE "21" CLUB IN NEW YORK CITY is my favorite restaurant in the entire world. When my husband was born, the owner sent his parents a silver lighter, and his uncle's racing colors adorn one of the jockey statues at the entrance of the building. I love the food, the service, and the ambience. I invariably choose the chicken hash for lunch and the steak Diane, prepared at the table, for supper. Here is a pared-down version of this jaw-droppingly rich classic dish.

6 tablespoons butter
6 tablespoons chopped shallots
4 8-ounce sirloin steaks, trimmed and pounded thin
2 tablespoons brandy or Cognac
1 teaspoon Worcestershire sauce, or to taste
Minced fresh flat-leaf parsley
Salt and pepper to taste

In a heavy skillet, melt 4 tablespoons of the butter and sauté the shallots. When the shallots are golden, add the steaks to the skillet over medium-high heat. Sear them quickly on both sides.

Add the brandy (it will flame up, which is part of the floor show). After the alcohol burns off, add the Worcestershire sauce and a few pinches of minced parsley. Stir in the remaining 2 tablespoons of butter. Season with salt and pepper and continue to sauté for another minute or so, until the steaks are cooked to your desired level of doneness. SERVES **4**

slob smarts Slash the fat on the edge of a steak at about 1-inch intervals to keep the meat from curling while it is on the grill.

steak au poivre

STEAK AU POIVRE is a classic French bistro staple, but you don't have to jig out to a swanky restaurant in order to enjoy it. This version can be created in less than twenty minutes and will be a great boost to your culinary self-esteem.

- **2 tablespoons cracked (not ground) peppercorns**
- **1 2-inch-thick shell (New York strip) steak**
- **2 tablespoons butter**
- **1 shallot, chopped**
- **1/4 cup heavy cream**
- **1 jigger Cognac**

Press the peppercorns into both sides of the steak. Place a cast-iron skillet over high heat.

After the pan heats up, add the steak. It will sizzle; don't worry. Cook for about 3 minutes; flip it once, and cook for 2 to 3 minutes on the other side for medium-rare, or to desired doneness.

Remove the steak from the pan, reduce the heat to medium, and toss in the butter. When it melts, sauté the shallots for 1 minute, then add the cream and Cognac. Stir, bring to a boil, then pour over the steak. SERVES **1**

My favorite animal is steak.

—FRAN LEBOWITZ

steak salad a mañana 

LEFTOVER STEAK makes great sandwiches, grilled with blue cheese. My husband also grills up extra cow so I can make this marinated steak salad the following day for lunch.

• • •

Slice the steak into matchstick-size pieces (about 1 cup of steak). Add 1 small onion, thinly sliced, and 4 carrots, peeled and chopped into matchsticks. If you feel like it, add 2 tomatoes or a few stalks of celery. In a small bowl, whisk together 1/2 cup of teriyaki sauce (2 tablespoons honey, juice of 1 lime, 3 tablespoons sesame seeds, 1 teaspoon minced ginger, and 2 tablespoons olive oil). Pour over the steak and vegetables and marinate for at least 30 minutes or up to 24 hours.

SERVES **4**

We didn't fight our way up the food chain in order to become vegans.

—ANONYMOUS

LIGHT-MY-FIRE BARBECUE BITES

- **Three out of four U.S. households own a barbecue grill. Sixty-one percent of grill owners have a gas grill. Eighteen percent own both a gas and a charcoal grill. Although men do the grilling duty in 66 percent of households, more women decide what foods to grill. Nearly 60 percent of grills are used year-round.**
- **Set your grill in a well-ventilated area, clear of trees.**
- **Before cooking on the grill, brush the cooking surface with oil so foods don't stick.**
- **Keep a spray bottle of water nearby to extinguish any flare-ups and use sturdy, long-handled tools.**
- **On an outdoor grill, meat should be grilled about 6 inches from the heat.**

BIGGER IS NOT ALWAYS BETTER

My friend Jim Csarneki grew up in a small town in central Pennsylvania called Clearfield. In his hometown, there is a restaurant called Denny's Beer Barrel Pub, home of the world's biggest burger, called the Ye Olde 96'er. Weighing in at 9 pounds, it contains 96 ounces of beef, 2 tomatoes, one-half head of lettuce, 12 slices of American cheese, 1 cup of sliced peppers, and 2 onions, plus condiments—mayonnaise, ketchup, and mustard. The meat alone is approximately 10,000 calories. They say no one has finished one yet.

just a regular hamburger 

THE TRICK TO THESE BURGERS is a hidden nugget of butter that keeps them juicy. If you feel like getting fancy, make a compound butter by mixing softened butter with garlic or your favorite herbs and seasoning. A neighborhood joint in Westwood, New Jersey, the Iron Horse, shoves chunks of cheese inside the burger patties, then grills them to perfection.

¼ pound coarse-ground beef
Butter
Salt and pepper

Shape the ground beef into a patty. Take a teaspoon-size knob of butter and slip it into the center of the burger, covering it entirely. Season with salt and pepper. Grill or fry in a cast-iron skillet to desired doneness. SERVES **1**

slob smarts My friend Scott has an indoor grill contraption so he can grill meat in his living-room fireplace. I guess he must really enjoy cooking to dirty up another room for preparing a meal. In my opinion, a kitchen is almost one room too many for cooking.

I will gladly pay you Tuesday for a hamburger today.

—WIMPY

aida turturro's meatballs 

AIDA TURTURRO IS A BEAUTIFUL WOMAN, a lavishly talented actress, a loving friend, and a spectacular cook. I have learned so much from Aida about generosity, strength, and cooking. Here is her famous meatball recipe. She insists that you have to be gentle with the ingredients, and not overwork them, so remember that. Aida knows what she is talking about. Serve these with marinara sauce over pasta or in a hero roll for a meatball sandwich.

1 pound ground beef
2 slices white bread, moistened with a few tablespoons of milk
1 cup grated Parmesan cheese
1 egg
Pinch of nutmeg
Olive oil, for frying

In a large bowl, mix together the ground beef, bread, Parmesan, egg, and nutmeg, using your hands. In a deep, heavy skillet, heat 1/2 inch of oil until quite hot. Roll the meat mixture into 1-inch balls. Fry in the olive oil. MAKES ABOUT **25** SMALL MEATBALLS

slob smarts Place a marble-size bit of cheese (blue, Cheddar, Brie) in the center of each meatball. Fry as above, and serve on cocktail picks as hors d'oeuvres. I keep resealable plastic bags of premade meatballs in the deep freeze ready to heat up in the oven. Just put them on a baking sheet right from the freezer and bake for 40 minutes at 350°F.

good old meat loaf

Nothing fancy here—just like Mom made, if she was partial to Italian sausage.

- 1½ pounds ground beef
- 1 pound hot or sweet Italian sausage, removed from the casing
- 1 medium onion, chopped
- 1 egg
- ½ cup fresh bread crumbs or 2 slices of stale bread soaked in a few tablespoons of milk
- Ketchup

Preheat the oven to 350°F.

In a bowl, mix together the beef, sausage, onion, egg, and bread crumbs. Use your hands to mix it all together. Pat it into a loaf shape on a baking sheet. Pour a few tablespoons of ketchup over the top. Bake for 50 minutes, or until done.

slob smarts While you're at it, toss a few potatoes and a bag of baby carrots in another baking dish and roast with olive oil and herbs.

Beef is the soul of cooking.

—Marie-Antoine Carême

meat-loaf mice 

WHEN YOU TELL PEOPLE that you are working on a cookbook, lots of them share opinions and recipes. My friend Lynn, who is a font of wisenheimer wisdom, suggested I include this variation on meat loaf. Perhaps I would have been more receptive during the initial pitch if it had a less verminesque name. I ultimately relented because when I made it for my godson, Eammon, he loved it. He also loved that I told him mice poop two hundred times a day. He is five. On the other hand, my husband's grandmother caught me making this, and she found both the idea and the execution revolting, so know your audience.

• • •

Using your favorite meat loaf recipe or the one on page 127, shape the mixture into 6 little mouse-size ovals on a baking sheet. Pop into a 375°F. oven for 35 to 40 minutes. When they are done, cut slices of carrots for ears, black olives for eyes, and pieces of uncooked spaghetti for whiskers.

If you are inspired, add pine nuts for teeth, and a caper for a nose. I bet if you put a tiny wedge of cheese on the plate, the mouse would eat it. SERVES **6**

slob smarts If the idea of reshaping meat back into animal shapes sets you on edge, bake individual meatloaves in a muffin pan. Top them with tomato sauce, mushroom gravy, or a sprinkling of grated cheese.

beef stroganoff

I RETURN TO THIS RECIPE whenever the weather turns cold. Although it has a fairly long cooking time, it is not active cookery; you just let it simmer away on top of the stove. While the Stroganoff is fending for itself in the kitchen, you can jig upstairs to paint your nails or give yourself a facial. When the Stroganoff is finished, serve it over egg noodles or mashed potatoes—extra credit if you garnish with chopped fresh parsley.

1½ pounds sirloin, cut into 1-inch strips
¼ cup flour
10 tablespoons (1¼ sticks) butter
1 cup chopped onion
1½ cups sliced mushrooms
1 cup beef broth
1 cup sour cream

Coat the strips of sirloin with flour. In a large sauté pan, melt 4 tablespoons of butter. Brown the sirloin strips in batches, adding up to 4 more tablespoons of butter as needed. Set the meat aside. In the same pan, sauté the onion and mushrooms in the remaining 2 tablespoons of butter until softened and lightly browned.

Add the meat and broth and bring to a boil.

Reduce the heat, cover, and simmer for 30 minutes. Stir in sour cream and let it heat through. SERVES **6**

The way you cut your meat reflects the way you live.

—CONFUCIUS

roasted pork tenderloin 
with garlic rub

PORK TENDERLOINS ARE AVAILABLE in most markets, and some even come packed in marinade. They are simple to prepare; just season with a wet or dry spice rub (see pages 156–157) and roast in a 450°F. oven for 10 minutes on each side. They are boneless and trimmed of excess fat, so there is no waste.

I like to serve roasted pork tenderloins when we invite guests to our farm for the weekend. They are great warm from the oven for those guests who arrive on time. For those caught in traffic, the meat stays moist and tender even if it has to be held for a few hours. My sister Kate gave me this simple recipe, which she makes the night before a big holiday get-together.

• • •

Preheat the oven to 450°F. Trim two 1-pound pork tenderloins. Mash 4 garlic cloves with kosher salt, then add pepper and chopped rosemary leaves to taste. Add about 2 tablespoons of olive oil to the mixture, so you can smear it all over the meat.

Place the tenderloins next to each other in a 9 × 13-inch roasting pan inside the oven. Roast for 10 minutes, then turn the meat over and roast for another 10 minutes, or until done. SERVES **6**

slob smarts If food has burned onto a pot or skillet, add about a tablespoon of baking soda to the soaking water.

> A little garlic, judiciously used, won't seriously affect your social life and will tone up more dull dishes than any commodity discovered to date.
>
> —ALEXANDER WRIGHT, *HOW TO LIVE WITHOUT A WOMAN*, 1937

dr pepper ham

THE DR PEPPER COMPANY is the oldest major manufacturer of soft-drink concentrates and syrups in the United States. The spicy-sweet soda cooks down to form a glaze over the ham. And just so you know, Coca-Cola contained cocaine until the beginning of the last century, and 7 Up contained lithium. Its slogan was "7 Up takes the ouch out of the grouch." This is a great recipe to feed a crowd, and it doesn't need a lot of attention from the cook.

- 1 10-pound precooked ham (not canned)
- 1 20-ounce bottle Dr Pepper
- 1 tablespoon dry mustard
- 1 cup dark brown sugar
- 1 tablespoon whole cloves

Preheat the oven to 350°F.

Put the ham in a roasting pan and pour the soda over it. Bake for 2 1/2 hours, basting with the pan juices.

Remove the ham from the oven and cut a diamond pattern onto the top. Mix the mustard and brown sugar, and rub into the hot ham. Stud the center of the diamond pattern with whole cloves. Return to the oven and bake for 30 more minutes. SERVES UP TO **20**

slob smarts Nodine's Smoke House will ship ham and other smoked meats right to your door: www.nodinesmokehouse.com.

niki lambros's
greek-style roast lamb

ONE EVENING I INVITED MY HUSBAND'S FAMILY over to our apartment for dinner. It was a special occasion and I used his grandmother's recipe for their favorite roast lamb. As the lamb roasted in the oven, I channeled June Cleaver and changed into a beautiful dress, pearls, and heels. I slipped an apron on over my dress and continued with the dinner prep.

Niki, John's grandmother, arrived first. I welcomed her into the living room, where we enjoyed a glass of wine. My husband arrived a bit later and when he saw me, his eyes nearly flew out of his head, and he asked to see me in the kitchen. "What do you have on?" he hissed. I looked down and realized the apron I had slipped on was an X-rated one I had received as a gag gift. To put it politely, it was a drawing of a well-endowed Italian gentleman, in a most excited state. The caption proudly boasted "Now *that's* Italian!" as he grabbed his enormous manhood. So much for good first impressions. At least the lamb was terrific.

5- to 6-pound leg of lamb, butt end
6 garlic cloves, chopped
Coarse salt
2 tablespoons olive oil
Pepper
Juice of 1 lemon
2 teaspoons dried Greek oregano
2 tablespoons fresh or dried rosemary

Trim the excess fat from the meat, or ask your butcher to do it for you.

With a mortar and pestle or in a small bowl with a wooden spoon, crush the garlic with some coarse salt to make a paste.

Preheat the oven to 400°F.

Cut slits into the lamb and push the garlic paste into them. Rub the oil onto the meat, then season with salt and pepper and lemon juice. Sprinkle with the oregano and rosemary. Place the lamb on a rack in a roasting pan.

Roast the lamb for 15 minutes, then reduce the heat to 350°F. Roast for about an hour, until the internal temperature of the lamb reaches 130°F.

Let the roast stand for 10 minutes before carving. Pour off the pan juices into a pitcher and serve on the side. SERVES **6** TO **8**

slob smarts Keep an aloe plant in the kitchen under the windowsill in case of minor burns.

Rosemary is a symbol of remembrance, because it was once thought to cure forgetfulness. I read that somewhere, but I forget where.

—ME

broiled lamb chops 

THE ONLY DOWNSIDE to this easy, easy recipe is that lamb can be expensive—but that didn't bother Shari Lewis, now did it?

- ¼ cup olive oil
- Juice and zest of 1 lemon
- 8 1-inch-thick lamb rib or loin chops

Preheat the broiler for 5 minutes. In a small bowl, mix together the oil, lemon juice, and zest. Brush the lamb chops with the olive oil–lemon marinade.

Place the chops on a roasting pan and broil them 4 inches from the heat for 5 to 6 minutes per side. SERVES **4**

slob smarts Chances are your stove has four burners. If you do the math you'll realize you don't need ten pots and pans cluttering up your cupboards, and you probably use the same favorites every day. Store the others, like your turkey roaster and that unused wok, in the basement or underneath your bed and free up some kitchen space.

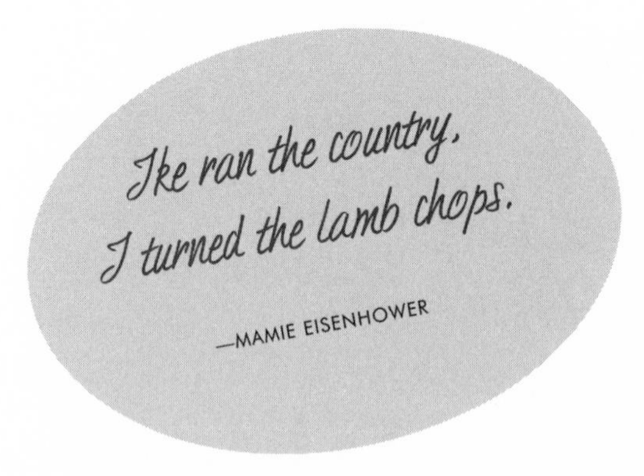

veal scaloppine

A WORD ABOUT BREAD CRUMBS. Have you ever tasted a spoonful of the packaged stuff sold in cardboard cylinders? Just thinking about it gives me the creeps. It is full of preservatives; it must have the shelf life of a book. Buy fresh bread crumbs from a bakery, or else make your own by grinding up heels and crusts, and store them in a resealable plastic bag in the freezer. If you feel like seasoning them, tailor the seasonings to what you are making. In a pinch, buy a package of stuffing mix and grind it up in a food processor or blender.

- 1 egg
- 1 cup bread crumbs, preferably fresh
- 1½ pounds veal cutlets, pounded thin
- 2 tablespoons butter
- 2 tablespoons olive oil
- ¼ cup chopped fresh flat-leaf parsley
- 1 lemon, sliced

In a shallow dish, mix together the egg and 2 tablespoons of water. Put the bread crumbs in another dish. Dip the veal cutlets first into the egg mixture, then into the bread crumbs.

In a skillet, melt 1 tablespoon of the butter; add 1 tablespoon of the oil. Pan-fry each cutlet for 2 to 3 minutes on each side. Add more butter and oil to the skillet in equal amounts as needed to prevent the cutlets from sticking.

Place the cooked cutlets on a warmed serving platter and cover with chopped parsley and lemon slices. SERVES **4**

slob smarts Bread crumbs? Grind some dry unsweetened cereal like cornflakes, Rice Krispies, or oatmeal in a blender (add salt, pepper, and herbs to taste), and use the crumbs as a substitute, or—in most cases—an improvement.

gravy-scented candles

IN MY NEIGHBORHOOD there is a tiny shop that sells candles the size of shot glasses at terrifyingly high prices. You pay more than fifty bucks to make your home smell like currants, pine, or the ocean.

Some of the bestselling candle fragrances are rose, gardenia, and pine, but none of these is a great complement to a savory meal. It gave me the idea to create a candle fragrance that would not cover up cooking odors but would in fact mimic kitchen activity. When I come in from a long day at work, I spark up a gravy-scented candle and order in Chinese food. It makes the house smell as if I have been cooking, when in fact I have been napping on the couch. When my husband walks in and says, "Honey, I'm sorry I'm late; did you cook dinner?" I can honestly reply, "You can smell, can't you?"

• • •

Spread newspaper over a work area.

Tie a length of wick to a pencil and suspend it across the top of a small Mason jar. Affix the wick to the bottom of the jar with a bit of melted wax. Repeat with 2 or 3 more jars and wicks.

Heat 1 pound of beeswax in a double boiler over low heat, stirring gently with a wooden spoon. Once the wax has melted, toss in a few brown crayons for gravy color and an envelope of packaged gravy seasoning. Stir gently to allow the color and scent to blend.

Using an oven mitt, lift the double boiler out of the water and slowly pour the melted wax into the jar until they are about three-fourths full. Allow the candles to harden; remove the pencil and trim the wick. Voilà—gravy-scented candles! MAKES ABOUT **5** 8-OUNCE JAR CANDLES

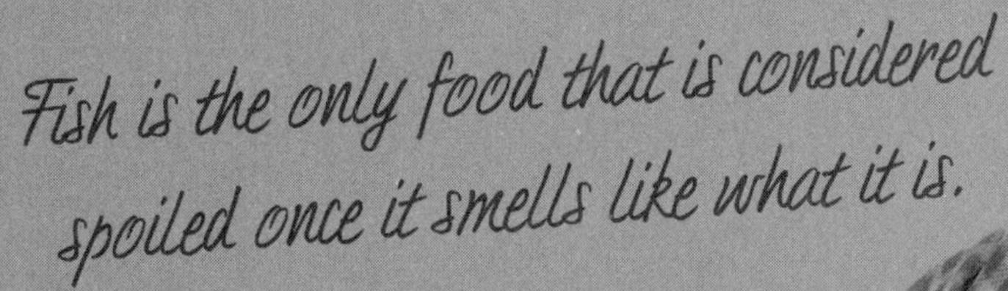

P. J. O'ROURKE

fish stories

aren't you smart to

serve fish tonight?

FISH IS THOUGHT OF as brain food, and who couldn't use some cerebral nourishment? **For a food known to make one smart, it is stupidly easy to prepare.** Right after graduating from college, I got a coveted job as an oyster shucker at the Fulton Street Café at the South Street Seaport in New York City. **Every morning, I would rise with the sun, load up the fish truck in New Jersey** with a salty dude named Fee, and deliver raw oysters, and clams, and crab, shrimp, eel, and fresh fish to the market. Fee and the fellas would unload the truck while I set up my little raw-bar cart. The South Street Seaport is in downtown Manhattan, not far from the financial district. At the time the economy was booming and hordes of hungry brokers and bond traders swarmed my cart.

Although I possessed an entrepreneurial spirit, **I was not**

blessed with the precise dexterity a good oyster shucker needs to keep up with tides of customers. Every lunch and happy hour, when I became buried in oyster orders, I would redirect the customers by saying, "Look, I'll shuck your oysters, but I drove them up from New Jersey myself. We may be talking hepatitis on the half shell. Why don't you try a few dozen shrimp?" That usually did the trick, of course, and the customers had to peel the shrimp themselves.

My career as a fishmonger lasted three seasons, and **I still have an enduring passion for *poisson*.** I do hope you take a crack at these fish dishes, and I encourage you to visit your local fishmonger. He or she will direct you to the freshest varieties and can give you some ideas on how to prepare them.

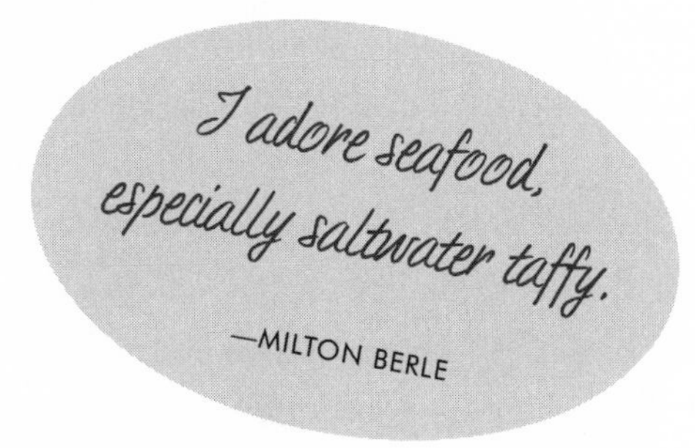

roasted oysters 

If you're one of those who shirk their fish-cooking duties because you think the house will smell like fish, allow me to retire that excuse. Grilled fish looks great and tastes fantastic, and only your downwind neighbors will have to worry about any lingering aromas.

. . .

Place fresh oysters in their shells on a hot grill. The heat will steam open the shells and gently poach the meat. Serve with lemon wedges and a bottle of Tabasco. No shucking required.

grilled fish

If you're not a championship shucker, your guests may starve to death before you get enough of these beauties open to feed your crew. This scrappy alternative will make your life much easier

. . .

For even cooking, choose pieces of fish that are the same size and thickness. Grill fish about 6 inches from the heat source. It cooks quickly and it is done when it loses it translucency; about 10 minutes per inch of thickness is a good rule of thumb. Check with the tip of a knife to see if it is opaque all the way through.

Cook very thin fillets on a pan over the grill, or on a piece of heavy-duty foil, so they won't fall through the grates. Don't try to flip thin fish fillets; they will just break apart. Cook on one side only.

slob smarts If storage space is limited, buy a baking sheet with sides (also called a half sheet pan) rather than a flat cookie sheet. It can be used for baking sheet cakes and for roasting vegetables, fish fillets, and shellfish.

salt and peppa shrimp 

THIS DISH PROVES THE RULE that you inevitably receive the greatest number of compliments for the dish that took the least time to prepare. Just smile graciously. Ask the fishmonger to devein the shrimp or else cut through the shell along the curved back with a paring knife and pick out the vein with a skewer.

- **3 pounds large shrimp, in the shells**
- **½ cup (1 stick) butter, cut into small pieces**
- **1 teaspoon kosher salt**
- **2 tablespoons cracked black pepper**
- **2 garlic cloves, minced**
- **French bread, for dipping**

Preheat the oven to 350°F.

Rinse and drain the shrimp and pat dry with paper towels. Place them in a baking dish and dot with the butter. Sprinkle with the salt, pepper, and garlic and bake for 15 minutes. Turn over the shrimp with tongs, and cook for 5 more minutes, or until opaque.

Pour the shrimp and the sauce into a deep platter and serve with a loaf of French bread for dipping in the sauce.

slob smarts The three most popular types of seafood in the United States are canned tuna, shrimp, and salmon.

I think somebody should come up with a way to breed a very large shrimp. That way, you could ride him, then, after you camped at night, you could eat him. How about it, science?

—JACK HANDEY

grilled shrimp shish kebabs 

TABASCO SAUCE HAS BEEN INCLUDED in the U.S. military's MRE (meals ready to eat) since before Operation Desert Storm. The standard military issue of Tabasco sauce is a 1/8-ounce bottle, easily stored on the battlefield. The McIlhenny Company, makers of Tabasco, published the *Charlie Rations Cookbook* and sent it to U.S. soldiers in Vietnam, along with a bottle of sauce. The cookbook, dedicated to the "battlefield gourmet," included some of the following recipes: Foxhole Hash, Combat Canapés, Ceasefire Casserole, Battlefield Birthday Cake, and Chicken Under Bullets.

This shrimp has a very gentle flavor; it's the Tabasco that adds the kick.

Use thin metal skewers, or soak bamboo skewers in premade margarita mix for 30 minutes before using (this prevents burning and gives a slap of flavor).

½ cup olive oil
¼ cup Authentic Cuervo Margaritas
Juice of 1 lime
2 teaspoons crushed red pepper flakes
Dash of Tabasco sauce
4 tablespoons chopped fresh flat-leaf parsley
2 pounds medium shrimp, drained and deveined

In a resealable bag, mix together the olive oil, margaritas, lime juice, red pepper flakes, Tabasco, and parsley. Toss in the shrimp and marinate in the refrigerator for 1 hour.

Thread the shrimp onto skewers. Place the skewers on a medium hot grill and cook, turning once, for about 3 minutes on each side, until the shrimp are cooked through. SERVES **4**

Even a fish wouldn't get into trouble if he kept his mouth shut.

—ANONYMOUS

lime-marinated swordfish 

SINCE OUR OCEANS are suffering from overfishing, check with your fishmonger about certain breed shortages. There have been warnings about swordfish and cod. This recipe can be adapted and used with any meaty, thick white fish steaks.

- Zest and juice of 3 limes
- 1/4 cup olive oil
- Dash of Tabasco sauce
- 4 swordfish steaks

In a plastic food storage bag or in a bowl, mix the lime zest and juice, oil, and Tabasco. Add the fish and marinate in the refrigerator for 1 hour.

Place the fish on a broiling pan and broil, or grill it in a grill pan on the stovetop or on a foil-covered outdoor grill.

Cook for about 5 minutes on each side, depending on thickness of steaks; don't overcook. Swordfish is done when the meat is white and still moist. SERVES **4**

slob smarts To remove lingering fish odors from the kitchen, bake some orange peel in a pie plate in a 350°F. oven for 15 minutes.

Don't overcook fish.
Most seafood should be simply threatened with heat and then celebrated with joy.

—JEFF SMITH (THE FRUGAL GOURMET)

salt-cooked salmon 

THE MORE TIME AND ENERGY you put into a meal, the greater the chance your guests will spend their time discussing other great meals they have enjoyed.

Adding a layer of salt to a skillet provides a high-heat environment for cooking salmon and results in a texture that's firm yet moist—as moist as if the fish had been poached. It's crucial to use a cast-iron skillet, which is the only kind of pan strong enough to withstand the heat generated by salt.

- **¾-pound center-cut salmon fillet with skin**
- **2 cups kosher salt**
- **¼ teaspoon freshly ground black pepper**

Season the salmon with a little salt and the pepper. Pour the remaining salt into a large cast-iron skillet. Place the skillet over high heat until the salt begins to smoke.

Put the salmon, skin-side down, on the salt. Cover, reduce heat to medium-low, and cook for 10 minutes, or just until the salmon is no longer translucent. Remove from the heat. Lift the salmon fillet off the skin and serve. SERVES **2** TO **3**

slob smarts The expression "not worth his salt" originated in ancient Greece, where salt was traded for slaves.

salmon with ginger-soy sauce 

THE SALMON COOKS in less than 6 minutes, and that's more than enough time in the kitchen for me. Serve on a bed of couscous or rice.

- 4 salmon fillets, about 5 ounces per serving
- Salt
- 2 tablespoons olive oil, for searing

SAUCE

- 2 tablespoons peeled and minced fresh ginger
- Juice of 1 lime
- 1 tablespoon soy sauce
- ½ teaspoon Thai chili sauce
- ¾ cup olive oil

Rinse the salmon, pat it dry, and lightly season it with salt on both sides.

Heat the 2 tablespoons of oil in a nonstick pan over high heat. When the oil is hot, add the salmon and cook for 2½ to 3 minutes. Turn the fillets over with a spatula, using a gentle touch, and cook for 1 minute on the other side.

To make the sauce, in a small bowl combine the ginger, lime juice, soy sauce, and chili sauce and whisk until blended. Gradually whisk in the olive oil until emulsified. Spoon the sauce over the salmon.

SERVES **4**

slob smarts Food shopping with a cart burns approximately 202 calories an hour. If you fished for your dinner you would burn approximately 230 calories per hour.

blackened fish fillets 

THE DEFINING FEATURE of blackened fish isn't an ingredient, it is intense heat. High heat concentrates the flavor of spices and creates a crisp exterior on the fish. This really smokes up the kitchen. You can do it over a grill outside; just preheat the skillet over the grill. Cook the fish quickly; you don't want it to look like a charred log.

4 fish fillets, such as orange roughy, red snapper, or catfish, about 6 ounces each
3 tablespoons olive oil
3 tablespoons Cajun spice blend

Brush the fish fillets with olive oil and sprinkle with Cajun seasoning.

Preheat a cast-iron skillet over high heat for 5 minutes. Place the fish in the preheated skillet and cook for 1 or 2 minutes on each side, depending on the thickness of the fillets, until deeply colored on the outside and opaque all the way through. SERVES **4**

slob smarts Historically, fish was served with lemon not only for the fresh stab of citrusy flavor, but also for medicinal purposes. Lemon juice was considered strong enough to dissolve any bones a diner inadvertently ingested.

Govern a family as you would cook a small fish—very gently.

—CHINESE PROVERB

sole in herb butter 

BUTTER SCULPTURE IS THE HIGHLIGHT of the Minnesota State Fair. On opening day the newly crowned Princess of the Milky Way spends six hours having her likeness carved out of a ninety-pound block of grade-A butter. The butter sculpture booth is one of the most popular attractions, and following the fair the princess gets to take her butter sculpture home. Some princesses have served their butter sculpture at their wedding reception. With one princess butter sculpture you could make 2,160 servings of Sole in Herb Butter.

- ½ cup (1 stick) butter, softened
- 2 tablespoons chopped fresh flat-leaf parsley
- 1 tablespoon chopped fresh dill
- 1 tablespoon fresh thyme leaves
- Juice of 1 lemon
- 6 sole fillets, about 6 ounces each
- ¼ cup flour
- 3 tablespoons olive oil
- Salt and pepper
- Lemon wedges and flat-leaf parsley, for garnish

In a small bowl, mix the butter, parsley, dill, thyme, and lemon juice. Set aside.

Preheat the broiler and gently coat the fish fillets with a light dusting of flour, shaking off any extra. Place the fillets in a greased broiler pan and brush with olive oil. Sprinkle with salt and pepper.

Broil for 3 minutes, then spoon the butter mixture over the fillets and return to the broiler until the butter melts, about 1 more minute. Transfer the fish to serving plates, spoon the herb butter over the fish, and serve with lemon wedges and fresh parsley. SERVES **6**

beer-battered fish fillets 

FRIED FISH STINKS UP THE KITCHEN; there is nothing one can do about it, except maybe drink another beer.

- 1½ cups flour
- 1 teaspoon salt
- ¼ teaspoon pepper
- Dash of cayenne pepper
- Dash of dry mustard
- 1 tablespoon vegetable oil
- 2 eggs
- ¼ cup flat beer
- 4 cups vegetable oil, for deep-frying
- 1 pound fish fillets, such as cod or halibut
- Lemon wedges, for garnish

In a medium bowl, mix the flour, salt, pepper, cayenne, mustard, and 1 tablespoon oil until blended.

Beat the eggs in a cup and add to the flour mixture, then add the beer. Cover the bowl and allow to rest, covered, for at least 1 hour, or overnight.

Heat the oil for deep-frying to 350°F. Cut the fish fillets into single portions. Dip 2 into the batter and deep-fry until golden, about 5 minutes, turning once. Drain on paper towels and keep warm in a 250°F. degree oven until all the fish fillets are fried. Serve with lemon wedges. SERVES **2**

slob smarts The Penn Brewery Restaurant in Pittsburgh, Pennsylvania, brews its own beer and hosts cook-offs with all recipes containing beer. Last year's winner was Chicken Cordon Brew.

Hunger is the best sauce.

—CERVANTES

saucy spoonfuls

marinades, sauces,

and spice rubs

to spice up your life

IT IS NOT my vaulting ambition to be a gourmet cook, foodie, or chowhound. I just want to have some fun while I'm exiled to the scullery and then to expedite my departure therefrom. There is no easier way to infuse food with flavor than with a simple marinade, spice blend, or quick sauce. **You could whip up any of these with one hand tied behind your back and both eyes closed.**

Marinades impart flavor to foods, and they are an excellent medium for basting as you grill; they are an all-purpose flavor end run. Pour your marinade into a resealable plastic bag; add the meat, fish, vegetable, or poultry. **I bet even tofu would be worth eating if it swam in some marinade for a bit,** though I'll probably never find out. Allow 1 hour for fish fillets, vegetables, and skinless chicken to marinate in the refrigerator, and allow up to 24 hours for chicken with skin, lamb, pork, or beef. While it loiters in your refrigerator, the food will soak up the great complementary flavors of the marinade.

The tougher the meat, the more acidic the marinade should be. Citrus juice, vinegar, wine, yogurt, and buttermilk are all acidic and work as marinades for poultry. Add flavor with aromatic vegetables, such as minced garlic, onions, shallots, and ginger and with herbs and spices such as rosemary, tarragon, mint, curry, and cumin. Use your nose; smell the spices and herbs, and choose the ones that appeal most.

Salt and sugar as well as acids like citrus juice and vinegar increase the flow of saliva. In the right proportions, they open the taste buds. These two actions stimulate the appetite.

Tomatoes and oregano make it Italian; wine and tarragon make it French. Sour cream makes it Russian; lemon and cinnamon make it Greek. Soy sauce makes it Chinese; garlic makes it good.

—ALICE MAY BROCK

Salt intensifies the natural flavor of foods and can bind several flavors into a harmonious union. That's why a bit of salt in sweet dishes helps to heighten the sweetness.

The basic distinction between the herb and spice families is that herbs grow in temperate climates, while spices grow in the tropics.

Lemon and citrus juices enlarge and refresh the flavor of foods. Grated citrus zest contains aromatic oils. Squeeze the juice of a lemon over a piece of fish and it will brighten the flavor. If you add the grated zest to butter, the aroma and freshness will be combined because the intensity of the lemon flavor carried in the lemon oil is more lasting.

A well-made sauce will make even an elephant or a grandfather palatable.

—GRIMOD DE LA REYNIÈRE

shoe-leather marinade 

I MAKE THIS OFTEN. My friend Beautiful Jenny named it "Shoe-Leather Marinade," because an old boot would taste great if you marinated it in this mixture for an hour.

- **1 cup soy sauce**
- **1/4 cup honey**
- **1/4 cup oil**
- **1 tablespoon minced garlic**
- **1 tablespoon peeled and minced fresh ginger**

In a large bowl, whisk together all the ingredients until well combined. MAKES A SCANT 1 3/4 CUPS

garlic marinade

THIS IS just a basic ratio—make as much or as little as you like.

- **2 parts oil**
- **1 part vinegar**
- **1 garlic clove, crushed**
- **Salt and pepper to taste**

In a large bowl, whisk together all the ingredients until well combined.

slob smarts Don't bother peeling garlic cloves. Smash them with the back of a knife and the skins will pop right off. Remove any green shoots as they are bitter.

greek mint marinade 

HERE'S ANOTHER GREAT CHOICE for adding flavor to lamb, poultry, or fish.

Juice and zest of 1 lemon
2 tablespoons dried mint leaves
1/3 cup olive oil

In a small bowl, stir together all the ingredients. MAKES ABOUT 1/2 CUP

slob smarts You can dry your own herbs by placing them on a paper towel and zapping them in a microwave for 1 minute.

greek garlic yogurt marinade 

THIS WILL LIVEN UP CHICKEN and lamb.

2 garlic cloves, minced
1/4 cup olive oil
1/2 cup plain yogurt
Salt and pepper to taste

In a medium bowl, combine all the ingredients. MAKES 3/4 CUP

slob smarts When mincing garlic, sprinkle a small bit of salt on the cutting board. The salt will keep the garlic from sliding all over the counter and will make a paste.

lemon pepper marinade 

USE AS A MARINADE or sauce for meat, chicken, fish, vegetables, or tofu.

Juice and zest of 1 large lemon
¼ cup olive oil
1 tablespoon cracked black pepper

In a small bowl, whisk together all the ingredients. MAKES ½ CUP

gremolata

THIS FRESH-TASTING, lemony blend is a perfect complement to roasted chicken, meat, or fish.

½ cup flat-leaf parsley, chopped
1 tablespoon capers, chopped
1 tablespoon lemon zest

In a small bowl, mix together all the ingredients. MAKES ½ CUP

slob smarts Hang a new shoe bag on the inside of a kitchen or pantry door to store utensils, linen, spices, and kitchen equipment.

garlic herb rub

SPICE RUBS ARE A COMBINATION of dried herbs and spices, sometimes with a bit of oil added so the rub sticks to the food. They're called rubs because you rub them on the surface of the meat. You can apply your rub just before cooking to give a flavorful crust, or several hours ahead of time so the flavors can absorb into the food. They impart a strong kick of flavor to all kinds of meat.

Rub this paste on pork, lamb, poultry, beef, or fish before cooking.

- **12 garlic cloves, peeled and smashed with the back of a knife or fork and a bit of coarse salt**
- **1 tablespoon chopped fresh oregano**
- **1 tablespoon chopped fresh thyme**
- **½ tablespoon chopped fresh rosemary**
- **2 teaspoons ground black pepper**
- **¼ cup olive oil**

Using a mortar and pestle or a blender, mix together all the ingredients to make a rough paste. MAKES ½ CUP

slob smarts Many fresh herbs can be frozen. Rinse the leaves, then roll in a paper towel and tuck into a food storage bag.

Garlick hath properties that make a man winke, drinke and stinke.

—THOMAS NASHE

rosemary rub

FOR EXTRA FLAVOR, rub this on lamb, chicken, or pork loin before roasting. The amount of rub used to cover the meat is up to you, but a good rule of thumb is about 1 tablespoon of rub for every pound of meat.

- **1 tablespoon olive oil**
- **1 tablespoon lemon juice**
- **1 tablespoon chopped fresh rosemary**
- **½ teaspoon kosher or sea salt**

In a small bowl, mix together all the ingredients. MAKES A SCANT ¼ CUP

duff's roadkill helper

THIS IS MY world-famous spice rub. It makes everything you put it on taste like food. Use it to season chicken, fish, beef, lamb, and tofu. My friend Mitch makes big batches of this rub and bottles it in spice jars to give as holiday gifts.

- **4 garlic cloves, peeled, smashed, and chopped**
- **1 teaspoon dried oregano**
- **1 teaspoon dried rosemary**
- **1 teaspoon dried thyme**
- **½ teaspoon black pepper**
- **½ teaspoon sea salt**
- **1 teaspoon freshly grated lemon zest**

In a small bowl, mix all the ingredients well. Refrigerate in a jar for 2 to 3 weeks. MAKES ABOUT ¼ CUP

whole cranberry sauce 

THIS IS ANOTHER RECIPE I heard on the Joan Hamburg radio program. Even if you don't like cranberry sauce, you'll probably like this. It puts the canned gelatin dreck in short pants.

- 1 12-ounce package whole cranberries, rinsed and picked over
- 1 cup orange juice
- ½ cup sugar
- 1 teaspoon vanilla extract
- ½ cup pecans

In a saucepan, simmer together the cranberries, orange juice, sugar, and vanilla for 15 minutes. Add the pecans and simmer for 5 more minutes, until the sauce is somewhat thickened. Serve warm or chilled. MAKES **2½** CUPS

peanut sauce 

SERVE WITH GRILLED SKEWERED chicken breast strips, or toss with noodles.

- 2 tablespoons vegetable oil
- 1 garlic clove, minced
- 1 teaspoon peeled and minced fresh ginger
- ½ cup smooth or chunky peanut butter
- 1 tablespoon soy sauce
- 1 tablespoon rice vinegar
- Cayenne pepper, if you are the spicy type

In a saucepan over medium heat, whisk together all the ingredients until the peanut butter melts and is blended in. MAKES ABOUT **½** CUP

olive tapenade

TAPENADE IS A RICHLY FLAVORED OLIVE SAUCE from the Provence region of France. Traditionally served on toast to accompany drinks, it is an excellent dip for vegetables or a no-cook sauce for fish or chicken.

- **1 cup pitted green or black olives**
- **4 garlic cloves, minced**
- **1/4 cup olive oil**
- **Salt and pepper to taste**
- **Red pepper flakes, for heat, if desired**

In a blender, by hand with a good knife, or with a mortar and pestle, blend, chop, or mash the olives, garlic, and olive oil to make a paste. Season with salt and pepper and with red pepper flakes, if desired.

MAKES **1** CUP

slob smarts Keep a few chopsticks handy in the kitchen. You can use them for mixing, stirring, and dislodging olives from the jar.

Condiments are like old friends—highly thought of, but often taken for granted.

—MARILYN KAYTOR

garlic mayonnaise

SERVE AS A SANDWICH SPREAD, with raw vegetables, or on grilled or broiled fish.

- 3 garlic cloves, minced
- 3/4 cup prepared mayonnaise
- 2 tablespoons olive oil
- 2 teaspoons lemon juice

In a medium bowl, combine the garlic and mayonnaise. Whisk in the olive oil a little bit at a time. Whisk in the lemon juice. MAKES ABOUT 1 CUP

Mayonnaise: One of the sauces
which serve the French
in place of a state religion.

—AMBROSE BIERCE

vegged out

the recipes

in this chapter

have been tested

on animals

You don't have to cook fancy or complicated masterpieces—just good food from fresh ingredients.

—JULIA CHILD

THE VIENNA VEGETABLE Orchestra was comprised of twenty musicians who performed on instruments created out of carrots, eggplants, pumpkins, and other vegetables. After their performances, cooks turned the instruments into soup for the musicians and the audience to eat together. Maybe that's the only way Viennese parents could get their kids to eat their vegetables . . .

The average supermarket stocks more than two hundred varieties of fruits and vegetables, and until recently I didn't like many of them.

My friend Joanna reminded me that she once came to a dinner party at my house and I served roasted chicken and potatoes and placed plastic toy vegetables on the guests' plates. Things have vastly improved since then, but **I still have to force myself to eat vegetables sometimes.** The USDA recommends five servings of fresh fruit and vegetables a day as a part of a healthy diet. This would be okay if you liked eating them, but not everyone does. As Doug Larson once said, **"If green, leafy vegetables smelled as good as frying bacon, we would all be a lot healthier."** And I'm trying. Now quite often I will make a meat entrée and three vegetable side dishes for dinner (though at least one of them is likely to contain bacon).

Here are some of the best ways I know to serve vegetables so they get off the plate and into your guests' gullets. They'll feel healthy and you'll have done a good deed.

> Man's unenthusiastic attitude towards vegetables persisted almost until modern times. Few vegetables were eaten in the Middle Ages and even then reluctantly . . . Vegetable salads and fruits were never regarded as substantial and legitimate parts of the meal. They did not come into daily use until the eighteenth century.
>
> —MARK GRAUBARD, *MAN'S FOOD, ITS RHYME OR REASON,* 1943

steamed vegetables 

Steaming is one of the easiest ways to get cooked vegetables on the table. When properly steamed, they retain the most nutrients, flavor, and color. Steaming vegetables is almost labor-free (especially if you steam baby vegetables or prewashed and prechopped produce). A steamer basket costs only a couple of bucks, so if you don't have one, there's no reason not to buy one unless you like your broccoli mushy and bland.

This method is easier than falling off a barstool. Bring a few inches of water to a boil in a large pot. A pasta pot or a stockpot is perfect. Place the vegetables on a rack or a steamer basket positioned half an inch above the water. Cover with a lid and cook as indicated below. While the vegetables are floating above their pot of water, you have time to fix yourself a drink.

Serve the steamed vegetables with butter and a squeeze of citrus to wake up the taste.

Here are some approximate cooking times.

ARTICHOKE . . . . 20 TO 25 MINUTES
ASPARAGUS . . . . 8 MINUTES
BRUSSELS SPROUTS . . . . 8 TO 10 MINUTES
BROCCOLI . . . . 10 TO 12 MINUTES
CARROTS, SLICED . . . . 10 TO 15 MINUTES
CAULIFLOWER . . . . 6 TO 10 MINUTES
CORN ON THE COB . . . . . . 6 TO 10 MINUTES
GREEN BEANS . . . . 10 TO 15 MINUTES
PEAS . . . . 10 MINUTES
POTATOES . . . . 20 TO 25 MINUTES
SPINACH . . . . 3 TO 5 MINUTES
ZUCCHINI . . . . 5 MINUTES

These times produce tender vegetables. If you prefer more crisp steamed vegetables, test the vegetables about halfway through the cooking time.

asparagus greek style

THE ASPARAGUS PATCH in our garden is a testament to nature over nurture. If you have the patience to wait three years for your first harvest, the average asparagus patch will produce for fifteen years.

A member of the lily family, asparagus stalks can grow up to ten inches in a twenty-four-hour period. During late spring and early summer, we harvest asparagus every day and have it for lunch *and* dinner.

I have a pot specifically designed for steaming asparagus, but I much prefer this recipe that my husband's grandmother taught me. We eat our fill of it while asparagus in season so I'm not tempted to buy tinned or off-season stalks in the market at terrifyingly high prices.

• • •

Trim off the end of the asparagus stalks if they are tough.

Add a bit of olive oil to a skillet. Toss in a few cloves of chopped garlic and cook for a minute or two. Add the asparagus and cook over medium heat until tender.

It's perfect as is, but if you're the type to gild the lily, serve with lemon, or drizzle with a bit of vinaigrette. ALLOW ABOUT A QUARTER POUND PER PERSON.

slob smarts A car is described as a lemon if it looks good on the outside, but turns out to be a clunker. It is derived from the exterior beauty of a lemon, which conceals a sour interior.

artichokes with lemon butter 

ONE EATS AN ARTICHOKE by pulling the flesh off the leaves with the teeth. This would have been difficult for George Washington, who had his real teeth extracted. He had several sets of false choppers made out of hippopotamus ivory and cows' teeth. The false teeth were held in his mouth with metal springs, and they all were too big for his mouth, which created a peculiar expression. Pity; he missed some good eating.

• • •

Place artichokes—one per person—in a heavy, deep pot and cover about halfway with water.

Cook at a boil until the leaves pull away easily, about 30 minutes. Add more water if needed.

Serve with Lemon Butter, made by combining 1/2 stick of butter, melted, with the juice of 1 lemon. Some people prefer to dip the leaves into a mayonnaise sauce; see page 160.

slob smarts Castroville, California, is known as the Artichoke Capital of the World. Back when she was still known as Norma Jean Mortenson, Marilyn Monroe was crowned Artichoke Queen there in 1947.

Eating an artichoke is like getting to know someone really well.

—WILLI HASTINGS

baked acorn squash 

DURING THE HOLIDAY SEASON, don't overtax yourself in the kitchen. Baked acorn squash is a delicious and ornamental side dish that takes virtually no effort to prepare.

- **2 acorn squashes**
- **Juice of 1 lemon**
- **4 teaspoons butter**
- **4 teaspoons brown sugar**

Preheat the oven to 375°F.

Cut each acorn squash in half lengthwise and scoop out the seeds.

Line a baking dish with foil and arrange the squash cut-side up in the pan.

Squeeze the lemon juice over the 4 squash halves, and add 1 teaspoon of butter and 1 teaspoon of brown sugar to each half.

Bake for 45 to 50 minutes, until the squash is fork tender.

SERVES **4**

slob smarts To save time and energy, try to bake different foods together in the oven. Don't be dogmatic; if temperatures vary slightly, make adjustments in the timing.

Old people shouldn't eat health food. They need all the preservatives they can get.

—ROBERT ORBEN

vegetarian black bean burgers 

YOU COULD TOP THEM with cheese or bacon, except then they wouldn't be vegetarian, they would be edible.

- **1 15-ounce can of black beans, rinsed and drained**
- **1 cup cooked rice**
- **1 medium onion, chopped**
- **1 egg, beaten**
- **4 hamburger buns, toasted**

Mash the beans in a large bowl with a potato masher or wine bottle. Add the rice, onion, and egg and mix well. Form into 4 burgers.

In an oiled skillet, cook the burgers over medium heat until browned on each side, about 5 minutes. Serve on toasted buns. For extra credit, top with spicy salsa.

SERVES **4**

slob smarts

One method of cutting an onion without tears is to place a burning candle by the cutting board. The sulfuric compounds are burned off by the flame. When chopping onions, go ahead and chop more than you need, freeze the extra in labeled plastic bags, and use them in the future, without shedding a single tear.

roasted brussels sprouts 

EVEN IF YOU HATE BRUSSELS SPROUTS, force yourself to try them this way. I first had them at my husband's favorite swanky restaurant, Babbo. This is my adaptation.

- **10** **bacon slices, cut into ½-inch pieces**
- **2** **boxes frozen Brussels sprouts or 2 cartons fresh, bottoms trimmed**
- **¼** **cup olive oil**
- **4** **garlic cloves, minced**

Preheat the oven to 350°.

Fry the bacon pieces over medium-high heat until crisp. Drain on a paper towel. Steam the sprouts until just tender, then cut into quarters. Place in a baking dish with the olive oil, garlic, and bacon pieces and toss to mix. Roast for 25 to 30 minutes, until tender.

SERVES **6** TO **8**

slob smarts The best bacon ever smoked is available through mail order from Nodine's Smoke House. Their smoked meats are transcendent.

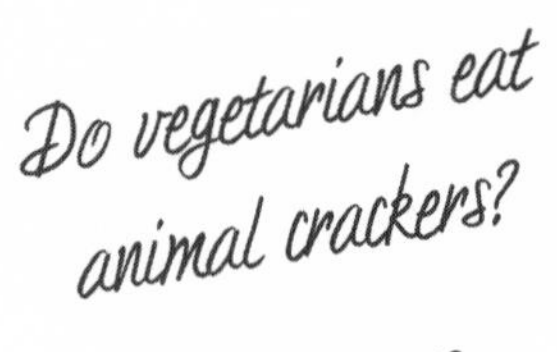

Do vegetarians eat animal crackers?

—ANONYMOUS

baked eggplant

- 2 tablespoons olive oil
- 1 medium eggplant, sliced ½-inch thick
- 1 medium onion, chopped
- 2 tomatoes, sliced
- 4 tablespoons freshly grated Parmesan cheese

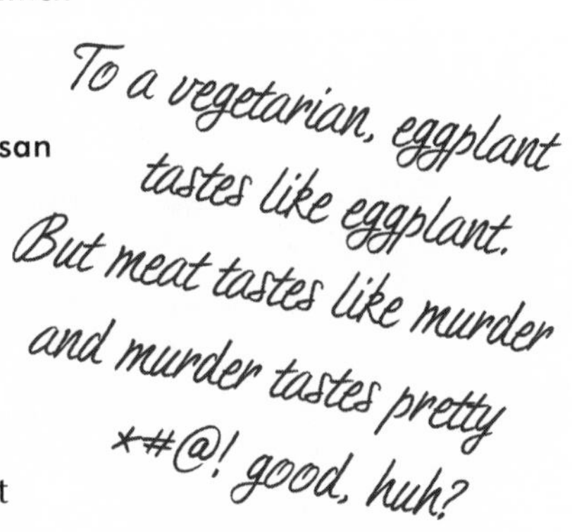

—DENIS LEARY

Preheat the oven to 375°F.

In a skillet, heat the oil and lightly brown the eggplant on both sides over medium-high heat. Remove the eggplant and sauté the onion until tender.

In a casserole dish or baking pan, layer the onion, eggplant, and tomatoes, in that order, making 2 or 3 layers of each. Sprinkle with the cheese and bake for 1 hour. SERVES **4**

dry-roasted cauliflower
with cumin

AN OLD EUROPEAN CUSTOM was that a soldier going off to war was given a loaf of bread seasoned with cumin baked by his fiancée. It was thought that cumin inspired faithfulness in men. What a crock! It does, however, do wonderful things to bland cauliflower. ONE MEDIUM HEAD WILL SERVE ABOUT **6**

• • •

Preheat the oven to 350°F.

Wash a head of cauliflower and cut into small florets. Dust the florets with cumin, set in a baking dish, and bake for 40 minutes, until tender.

Man, I love to cook. I love to hold a vegetable in my hand, an eggplant or a carrot or an onion. I love to slice it open, hear the sound as I cut through it, note the difference between the outside and the inside of it, see the beautiful patterns inside the seeds of the eggplant, the layers of the onion, the orange star flower pattern in a carrot. I love to beat and sift and stir and measure and pour. I love putting together all these good ingredients and watching them turn into something new.

—CRESCENT DRAGONWAGON, *THE COMMUNE COOKBOOK*, 1972

corn pudding

MY FRIENDS AIDA AND LIZZIE and I are a high-energy trio. Sometimes too much so. When the three of us tried to cheer up another pal who was in a tight spot, we arrived with a dish of corn pudding, a litany of opinions, and six shoulders to cry on. Slightly uplifted, our pal remarked that our efforts made her feel as if she had been "punched by an angel."

- **3 eggs**
- **1/8 teaspoon nutmeg**
- **2 tablespoons cornstarch**
- **1 cup milk**
- **1 16-ounce can cream-style corn**
- **2 tablespoons melted butter, plus cold butter to grease baking dish**

Preheat the oven 350°F.

In a mixing bowl, stir the eggs together with the nutmeg. Sprinkle in the cornstarch and beat with a whisk until smooth. Stir in the milk, corn, and melted butter.

Pour the pudding mixture into a greased baking dish and set the dish in a larger pan containing enough hot water to reach about one-third of the way up the side of the pan. Bake for about an hour, or until set and firm. SERVES **4**

slob smarts Use a large bowl as a refuse bin for eggshells, vegetable scrapings, and other assorted kitchen debris created as you cook. A garbage bowl at your workspace will spare you the added chore of cleaning up the bits you drop on the way to the kitchen garbage can. A good cook cleans as he or she cooks, but cooking creates the need to clean. It is a symbiosis, and a Sisyphean task.

corn al roker

BELOVED TELEVISION WEATHERMAN Al Roker is a casual acquaintance of mine. He is a sweetheart and one of the most positive, generous men in the world. One afternoon over lunch he gave me this recipe for corn on the cob. We call it Corn Al Roker.

In appreciation of this recipe, we sculpted a likeness of a pre-gastric-bypass-surgery Al Roker out of cheese and dubbed it Al Roquefort. My friend Mitch and I placed the cheese sculpture in a wagon and carted it over to Al at the TV studio. He seemed to like it.

. . .

Strip the husks and silk from the ears of corn. Wrap each naked ear in foil, and place on the grill for 20 to 30 minutes. That's it.

fried corn

Slice the kernels off some leftover corncobs. In a skillet, melt a bit of butter, add the corn, and cook over medium-high heat until warmed through. Season with salt and pepper and serve.

slob smarts The easiest way to strip a corncob of the annoying, flosslike silk is to rub a vegetable brush all over the corn under running water.

peas and mint

WINSTON CHURCHILL said, "We lived very simply here, but with all the essentials of life well understood and well provided for—hot baths, cold champagne, new peas and old brandy." Try these pea recipes and see for yourself why Winston loved them so much.

- **2 10-ounce packages frozen petite peas**
- **½ to 1 teaspoon minced fresh mint leaves**
- **2 tablespoons butter**

In a medium saucepan, cook the frozen peas according to package directions.

Drain off the water and add the mint and butter. Gently stir and shake the pan to mix well. SERVES **4**

peas and prosciutto

- **1 10-ounce package frozen petite peas**
- **1 tablespoon olive oil**
- **1 medium white onion, chopped**
- **4 slices prosciutto, chopped**
- **Salt and pepper to taste**

> All I'm saying is give peas a chance.
> —ANONYMOUS

Place the peas in a saucepan and cook according to package directions.

In a sauté pan, heat the olive oil and cook the chopped onion until tender, about 8 minutes. Add the prosciutto, and cook for 1 minute more. Drain the peas and stir in the onion and prosciutto mixture. Season with salt and pepper. SERVES **4**

slob smarts Frozen peas are essential in my household. I grow fresh peas in my garden, but I use frozen peas for the convenience. Even if you hate frozen peas, you can use the kind in a bag as an ice-pack hangover aid.

roasted garlic

ROASTING MELLOWS AND SWEETENS the flavor of garlic. Squeeze the soft cloves onto bread, meat, or vegetables. The medicinal benefits of garlic go well beyond vampire repellent.

- 1 head garlic
- Drizzle of olive oil

Preheat the oven to 350°F.

With a sharp knife, slice off the top of the garlic head to reveal most of the interior cloves. Place on a piece of aluminum foil and drizzle the top of the garlic head with a few drops of oil. Wrap the garlic in the foil and bake for about an hour. (You can also toss the garlic on a hot grill for 35 to 45 minutes.) The garlic is done when it feels soft when pressed with tongs.

roasted rosemary red potatoes

- 1 pound red new potatoes, scrubbed
- 1 tablespoon fresh or 1 teaspoon dried rosemary
- 4 garlic cloves, roughly chopped
- Salt and pepper to taste
- 1 tablespoon olive oil

Preheat the oven to 375°F.

In a baking dish, toss the potatoes with the rosemary, garlic, salt, and pepper. Drizzle with the olive oil. Roast for 30 minutes, or until slightly wrinkled and tender. SERVES **6**

baked potato chips 

ALTHOUGH A STEREOTYPICAL STAPLE of Irish cuisine, the potato is native to South America and was taken to Europe from Peru by Spanish conquistadores in the sixteenth century. These chips are delicious, and you won't look like an adolescent fry cook glistening with dermatological consequence after eating them.

• • •

Preheat the oven to 375°F.

Slice unpeeled potatoes very thin—1/8 inch or less. Dip each slice in melted butter and lay on a cookie sheet. Season with salt and your favorite seasoning, such as cayenne pepper or garlic.

Bake for 35 minutes, until tender. ALLOW ABOUT **1** MEDIUM POTATO PER PERSON—OR MORE IF YOU HAVE NO QUALMS ABOUT CARBS

slob smarts In the 1860s, all potato chips were known as Saratoga Chips. Legend has it that a hard-to-please guest at a restaurant in Saratoga Springs, New York, kept sending his order of oversize French fries back to the kitchen for further cooking. The chef, George Crumb, cut the potatoes into thin strips and boiled them in fat. The guest loved them, and chips have ultimately become one of the bestselling snack foods of all time.

baked french fries 

During Operation Enduring Freedom, the U.S. government renamed French fries "freedom fries." This type of foolishness is not unique to the Bush Republicans; in fact, during World War I sauerkraut was renamed "liberty cabbage" and frankfurters were called "liberty sausages" so housewives would not have to use the enemy's language when making dinner.

- 2 teaspoons paprika
- 1 tablespoon garlic powder
- 1 tablespoon onion powder
- ½ teaspoon pepper
- ½ teaspoon sea salt
- 6 baking potatoes

Preheat the oven to 400°F. Spray a baking sheet with cooking spray, or coat lightly with olive oil.

In a small bowl or resealable plastic bag, combine the paprika, garlic powder, onion powder, pepper, and sea salt.

Scrub the potatoes well, and cut into ½-inch strips. Toss the potatoes with the seasoning mix. Place the potatoes on the prepared baking sheet and bake for 30 minutes, turn the potatoes over, and bake for 20 minutes more. SERVES **6**

slob smarts Store potatoes in a cool, dry, dark place. Refrigerators have too much moisture and will wither them.

My favorite vegetable dishes are jellybeans, carrot cake, and sweet potato pie.

—ME

faster potato gratin

LIFE ISN'T WORTH A PLUGGED NICKEL if you resort to instant mashed potato flakes. What could you be doing that is so important that you can't eat a real potato? Try Faster Potato Gratin. Is it faster than a monkey on rocket skates? No, but I bet it tastes better. This expeditious version of the classic recipe elevates the humble potato to side-dish star status.

2 pounds all-purpose potatoes, peeled and sliced thin
Salt and pepper
1 teaspoon minced garlic, or a fine grating of nutmeg (optional)
2 tablespoons butter, cut into small pieces
2 to 3 cups half-and-half or milk

Preheat the oven to 400°F.

In a nonstick ovenproof skillet, layer the potatoes, sprinkling between the layers with salt and pepper, and garlic or nutmeg, if you like. Dot with the butter, then add enough half-and-half to come about three quarters of the way to the top.

Place the skillet on the stovetop over high heat, and bring the half-and-half to a boil. Reduce the heat to medium high and cook for about 10 minutes, or until the level of liquid reduces by about half. Transfer the skillet to the oven and cook until browned, about 10 minutes more. Serve or keep warm in the oven for up to 30 minutes.

SERVES **4** TO **6**

slob smarts During the Klondike gold rush in Alaska from 1897 to 1899, potatoes were so highly valued for their vitamin C content, gold miners traded potatoes for gold.

roasted mashed sweet potatoes 

ONE EASTER, a few friends and I made a beautiful holiday meal. We noticed that we had forgotten to dye the eggs, so instead we used food coloring to dye the food: bright blue mashed potatoes, purple turkey, red butter, and green cake. Yum.

3 medium sweet potatoes (9 ounces each), peeled and cubed
½ cup milk
¼ cup brown sugar
2 tablespoons butter
½ teaspoon salt
2 eggs, separated
20 marshmallows

Preheat the oven to 325°F. Grease a 6-cup baking dish.

In a saucepan, combine the sweet potatoes with water to cover. Bring to a boil and cook until tender. Drain the potatoes and mash until smooth. Stir in the milk, sugar, butter, and salt and cook over low heat until the butter melts. Gradually beat the egg yolks into the potatoes.

In a separate bowl, beat the egg whites until stiff. Fold into the potato mixture. Spoon the mixture into the baking dish and top with the marshmallows. Bake for 10 to 15 minutes, or until the marshmallows are melted and browned. SERVES **6**

slob smarts The sweet potato belongs to the same family as morning glories, while the white potato belongs to the same group as tomatoes, tobacco, chili peppers, eggplants, and petunias.

sautéed spinach

with lemon and garlic

SPINACH IS ONE of the most reviled vegetables, and served overcooked, it can be a most despondent example of chlorophyll. This method of spinach preparation takes less than 2 minutes, and the lemon juice and garlic enhance its taste so much that the vitamins can almost be overlooked.

1 pound spinach leaves, rinsed well, stems removed
1/4 cup olive oil
2 garlic cloves, minced
Juice of 1 lemon
Salt and pepper to taste

Toss the rinsed spinach (with water still clinging to the leaves) into a large skillet or sauté pan and cook over medium-high heat until wilted, 1 to 2 minutes. (Or you can microwave it for 1 minute.)

Transfer the spinach from the pan to a bowl while you heat the olive oil in the same skillet over medium-high heat. Add the garlic and cook until lightly golden. Add the spinach and lemon juice, stir well, and season with salt and pepper. SERVES **2**

slob smarts During World War II, wine was fortified with spinach juice and given to injured French soldiers.

There is no such thing as a little garlic.

—ARTHUR BAER

creamed spinach

AT LEAST ONCE A WEEK I make myself a big bowl of creamed spinach for lunch. One afternoon I ate such a big bowl that I had to say a prayer to Saint Emerentiana, the patroness saint of upset stomachs.

- **3 pounds fresh spinach, large stems discarded (or substitute 2 packages of frozen, just defrost it and squeeze it dry, then progress to the next step)**
- **1 teaspoon vegetable oil**
- **1 medium shallot, minced**
- **1 cup heavy cream**
- **4 tablespoons (½ stick) butter**
- **¼ cup freshly grated Parmesan cheese**
- **Salt and freshly ground pepper**

Heat a large saucepan. Add the spinach by the handful and cook over medium-high heat, stirring often, until it's all wilted, about 5 minutes. Transfer the spinach to a colander and when cooled, squeeze it as dry as possible. Chop the spinach.

Heat the oil in the same saucepan. Add the shallot and cook over medium heat, stirring, until golden, 4 to 5 minutes. Add the cream and cook until reduced by half, 6 to 7 minutes. Add the butter and swirl to incorporate. Stir in the Parmesan and cook over low heat for 2 minutes. Add the spinach and ¼ cup of water, season with salt and pepper, and cook over low heat until heated through. SERVES **6**

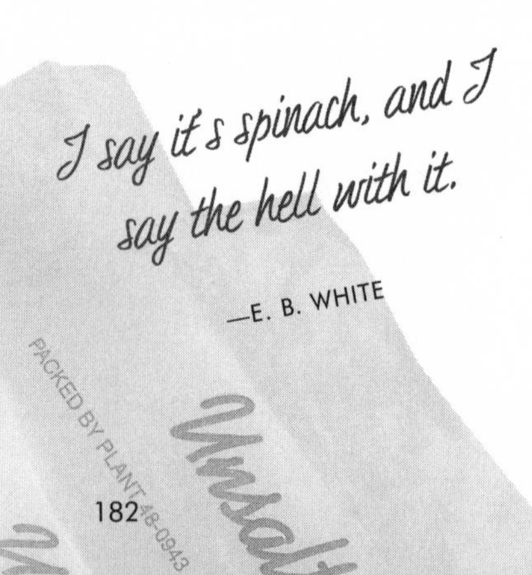

I say it's spinach, and I say the hell with it.

—E. B. WHITE

broiled tomatoes 

I INVITED MY HUSBAND'S GRANDMOTHER Niki to go produce shopping with me at the farmers' market. I was checking out a gorgeous display of organic tomatoes when Niki told me, "Honey, you are too old to start eating organic vegetables. For you it's too late; don't bother with the expense." I love old people.

• • •

Slice ripe tomatoes 1/4 inch to 1/2 inch thick. Splash them with a small amount of olive oil and sprinkle with a generous amount of freshly grated Parmesan cheese.

Run under a hot broiler until the cheese is melted and golden, 3 to 5 minutes, depending on how close the pan is to the heat.

2 BIG TOMATOES WILL SERVE **2** TO **4** PEOPLE, BUT MAKE LOTS. YOU'LL BE GLAD YOU DID.

slob smarts Each American eats approximately 22 pounds of tomatoes yearly, over half of that in the form of ketchup and tomato sauce.

Be careful with what you read in health books. You could die due to a misprint.

—MARK TWAIN

baked zucchini

with herbs and tomatoes

UNTIL THE NINETEENTH CENTURY, tomatoes, a member of the nightshade family, were considered poisonous. Some people still feel that way about zucchini, but baked this way it is extremely palatable.

- **10** firm baby zucchini, or 5 small zucchini, cut into ½-inch chunks
- **1** small onion, chopped
- **5** whole ripe plum tomatoes, cored and coarsely chopped
- Salt and pepper
- A few pinches of fresh or dried thyme
- **⅓** cup extra-virgin olive oil

Preheat the oven to 425°F.

Toss the zucchini, onion, and tomatoes in a bowl. Season with salt, pepper, and thyme. Pour half of the olive oil into a 2-quart baking dish. Add the vegetables, and drizzle the remaining oil on top.

Bake for 20 to 30 minutes, or until the vegetables are cooked and tender. SERVES **6**

slob smarts In a well-run grocery store, the freshest items will come from the back of the shelf. The average grocery store stocks more than two hundred varieties of fresh fruits and vegetables.

Without bread all is misery.

—WILLIAM COBBETT (BRITISH JOURNALIST, 1763?–1835)

breadwinners

forget the Atkins diet;

live your life

and bake some bread

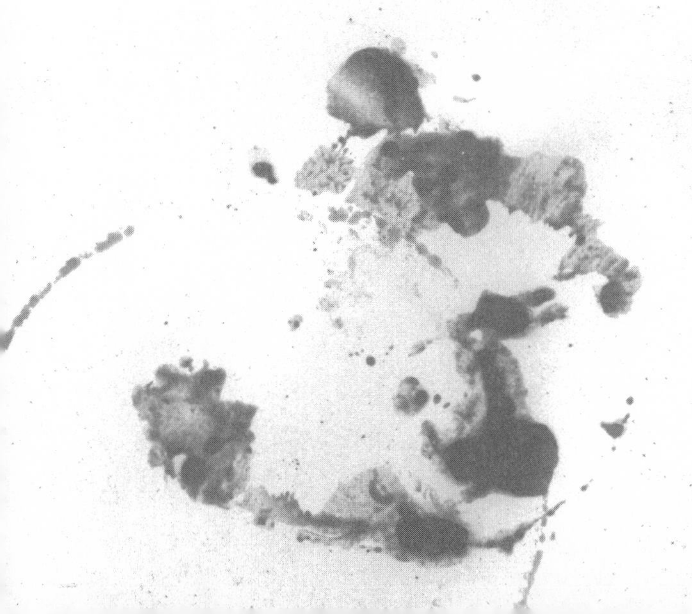

A recipe doesn't belong to anyone.
Given to me, I give it to you. It is
only a guide, a skeletal framework.
You must fill in the flesh according
to your nature and desire.

—EDWARD ESPE BROWN, *THE TASSAJARA BREAD BOOK*, 1970

WHEN I FLIP through cookbooks, I notice that **many of them are as overwritten as a bodice ripper.** Oven-roasted chicken? Hmm . . . I was thinking that instead of using the oven to roast it, I would just wrap it up in a sweater. For crying out loud. But it's the serving suggestions that really get my knickers in a twist: "Serve with a nice loaf of warm, crusty bread." **What do they think I am going to buy—a stale, old, crustless loaf?**

My sister Kate, who never made a muffin in her life, believes that certain things should be left to the professionals, like haircuts and bread baking. While I don't entirely agree with her, I am glad I don't have to slave over every crumb that goes into my family's mouths. **If I have learned anything about cooking, it's that there is no point in kicking up a fuss.** Why subject yourself to unnecessary frustration and irritation, on top of a big mess?

For those days when you just *feel* like baking bread—maybe it's a rainy afternoon, or you forgot to take your Ritalin—**here are a few bread recipes worth trying.** You are not going to win any bake-offs with these, but I bet your resourcefulness will win some admirers. I've included a few spreads, too, to gild your baked lily.

There are basically two types of bread: those leavened chemically (with baking powder), called quick breads, and yeast-risen breads. While I have only included one recipe for the latter, **don't be menaced by yeast; it's just a simple single-celled microorganism.** You are much more clever. You're not going to be pushed around by a single cell, are you?

SLOB SMARTS

Use a strand of uncooked linguini to test baked goods. Insert the linguine into the center of the baked item in question, then remove it. If the linguine comes out clean, the cake, muffin, or whatever is done.

sour-cream biscuits 

My collection of vintage community cookbooks, the spiral-bound volumes published as fund-raisers by civic-minded women's clubs, has yielded many surprises. Some, like the Chinese Haystacks (a can of chow mein noodles enrobed in melted butterscotch chips) are for more rarefied tastes. Others, like these sour-cream biscuits, have become a staple of my culinary repertoire. They are so simple, the only way to mess them up is to burn them.

1 cup self-rising flour
½ cup (1 stick) butter, melted
½ cup sour cream

Preheat the oven to 375°F.

In a medium bowl, combine the flour, butter, and sour cream and mix well. Drop by rounded tablespoons into a greased muffin tin or onto a greased baking sheet.

Bake for 15 to 20 minutes, until they puff up like Rosie O'Donnell and turn golden brown. MAKES ABOUT **A DOZEN** LOVELY BISCUITS

slob smarts *Biscuit* means "twice baked" in French.

baking-powder biscuits 

OKAY, THE NAME OF THIS RECIPE is Baking-Powder Biscuits. Despite that fact, when my friend Lynn and I were testing this recipe, we forgot to add the baking powder. They didn't rise, but they still tasted great. We simply renamed them "Self-Buttering Biscuits," and ate them right up. We like to make these with butter, but it's your choice.

- 2 cups sifted all-purpose flour
- 1 tablespoon baking powder (don't forget!)
- 1 teaspoon salt
- 1/3 cup butter or vegetable shortening
- 3/4 cup milk

Preheat the oven to 425°F.

In a mixing bowl, combine the flour, baking powder, and salt. Cut in the butter until the mixture looks like coarse meal. Add the milk and stir until blended.

Transfer the dough to a lightly floured surface and knead gently, about 10 times. Roll out the dough to 1/2-inch thick. Cut out biscuits with a floured biscuit cutter or juice glass. Bake on an ungreased baking sheet for 12 to 15 minutes. MAKES ABOUT **1 DOZEN** FLUFFY BISCUITS

slob smarts Measure out your baking ingredients and line them up on the counter. This will make it easier to follow the recipe, and you'll have a cleaner kitchen in the end.

beer bread

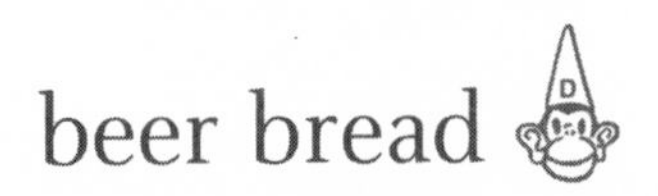

THE UNION OF THESE SIMPLE INGREDIENTS creates a perfectly passable loaf of bread, great for eating or tossing to the ducks. This bread is greatly improved if you throw in a cup of halved pitted olives, a cup of shredded cheese, or some chopped nuts.

12 ounces beer
2⅔ cups self-rising flour

Preheat the oven to 375°F. Lightly grease a 9 × 5 × 3-inch loaf pan.

In a medium bowl, combine the beer and flour, and mix well. Scrape the batter into the loaf pan and bake for 50 to 55 minutes. The top should be lightly browned, and the sides should pull away from the pan.

Cool for a few minutes, then remove the loaf from the pan and continue to cool on a rack. MAKES **1** LOAF

slob smarts Beer is defined as a staple food in Bavaria. Also, the most popular beverage in the world is tea, and beer is number two. In England and Ireland, however, beer is the most popular beverage.

Without bread, without wine, life is nothing.
—FRENCH PROVERB

irish soda bread

ONE AFTERNOON when my mom was coming to visit, I decided to make a nice loaf of Irish soda bread, one of her favorites foods. When she arrived, we sat in my kitchen while the bread baked and she confided that she hadn't had a happy childhood until she met my dad, and that it's never too late to have a happy childhood. One can have the most interesting conversations while bread is baking.

- 2 cups all-purpose flour
- ½ teaspoon baking soda
- 1½ teaspoons baking powder
- ½ teaspoon salt
- 1 tablespoon sugar
- 4 tablespoons vegetable shortening or butter (use whatever you have; either will work)
- ¾ cup buttermilk or sour milk (see Note)

Preheat the oven to 375°F.

In a large bowl, combine the dry ingredients and stir. Cut in the shortening. Stir in the buttermilk, and knead the dough with your hands to mix well.

Shape the dough into a round loaf about 1 inch thick and set it on a greased baking sheet. Bake for 30 minutes, or until a cake tester comes out clean. MAKES 1 LOAF

NOTE To make sour milk, add 1/4 cup vinegar to 3/4 cup milk and let sit for 5 minutes.

slob smarts Mix the batter just until the wet and dry ingredients are combined. Overmixing will develop the gluten in the bread, and make it tough and chewy.

zucchini bread

THERE IS A SAYING that if you don't receive any zucchini during the growing season, you don't have any friends. If someone drops off a basket of zucchini at your door, nick a package of corn-bread or bran-muffin mix and add a cup of shredded zucchini to the batter. Bake according to the directions on the package. Or you could immerse yourself in domestic loveliness and make this easy-to-prepare home-baked loaf.

- 3 cups shredded zucchini (3 medium-size zucchini)
- 1⅔ cups sugar (see Note)
- ⅔ cup vegetable oil
- 2 teaspoons vanilla extract
- 4 eggs
- 3 cups all-purpose flour
- 2 teaspoons baking soda
- 1 teaspoon ground cinnamon
- ½ teaspoon ground nutmeg
- ½ teaspoon baking powder

Preheat the oven to 350°F. Grease the bottoms only of two 9 × 5 × 3-inch loaf pans.

In a large bowl, mix the zucchini, sugar, oil, vanilla, and eggs. Stir in the flour, baking soda, cinnamon, nutmeg, and baking powder. Pour the batter into the pans. Bake for 50 to 60 minutes, or until a cake tester inserted in the center comes out clean. Let cool for 10 minutes. Loosen the sides of the loaves and remove from the pans.

MAKES **2** LOAVES

NOTE If you use half white and half brown sugar, it tastes even better.

pumpkin bread

EVERY FALL I INVITE a big group of girlfriends up to my farm for a Wild Women's Weekend during which we eat, drink, laugh, hike, shop, dance, and stay up all night. Some years I will hire a fortune-teller or a masseuse, and every year I ask my friend and cooking mentor, Beverly Morris, to help me plan, cook, and serve the meals. Everybody pitches in and the weekends are legendary. We have a few traditions: the interpretive dance competition; cocktails at a handsome, charming bachelor's swanky house; and sandwiches of pumpkin bread with cream cheese at tea time. I like to bake this bread in greased coffee cans. Fill the cans two-thirds full and stand the cans on a baking sheet. Bake as directed.

- 3 cups sugar
- 1 cup vegetable oil
- 4 eggs, beaten
- 1 16-ounce can pumpkin purée
- 3½ cups all-purpose flour
- 1 teaspoon baking soda
- 2 teaspoons salt
- 1 teaspoon baking powder
- 1 teaspoon ground nutmeg
- 1 teaspoon ground cinnamon
- 1 teaspoon ground ginger

Preheat the oven to 350°F. Grease and flour two 9 × 5 × 3-inch loaf pans.

In a large bowl, cream together the sugar and oil with a fork. Add the eggs and pumpkin and mix well.

In a separate bowl, sift together the flour, baking soda, salt, baking powder, nutmeg, cinnamon, and ginger. Add the dry ingredients to the pumpkin mixture, alternating with 2/3 cup of water, and mix well.

Pour the batter into the loaf pans. Bake for 1 1/2 hours, or until a toothpick or cake tester inserted into the center comes out clean and the tops of the loaves spring back when touched.

Let stand for 10 minutes, then remove from the pans to cool. Slice and smear with cream cheese. MAKES **2** LOAVES

1-2-3 POP! popovers 

THESE ARE GREAT to whip up when guests pop over. You can serve them with jam as a sweet, or with a quick soup.

- **2 eggs**
- **1 cup all-purpose flour**
- **1 cup milk**
- **1/2 teaspoon salt**

Preheat the oven to 450°F. Grease and flour six muffin cups or 6-ounce custard cups (or you could spring for a popover pan).

In a medium bowl, beat the eggs with a fork. Add in the flour, milk, and salt and beat until the batter is smooth. Don't go crazy; you want to blend the batter gently. Fill the greased and floured cups one-half full.

Bake at 450°F. for 20 minutes, then decrease the oven temperature to 350°F. and bake for another 20 minutes.

Pop the popovers from the cups and serve them piping hot with butter or jam. SERVES **6**

banana bread

If you don't feel like going through all the measuring and mixing, you can take a shortcut by opening a box of corn-bread mix or bran-muffin mix. Prepare it according to the directions on the package, then mash up a couple of overripe bananas from the fruit bowl, stir them in, and follow the baking instructions. If shortcuts present themselves, I suggest you fly when the window is open.

- 1½ cups all-purpose flour
- 1 teaspoon baking soda
- 1 teaspoon salt
- ⅓ cup vegetable oil
- ¾ cup brown sugar
- 1 cup mashed banana (2 to 3 very ripe bananas)
- 2 eggs, lightly beaten
- ⅓ cup milk
- ½ cup chopped walnuts or pecans

Preheat the oven to 350°F. Grease and flour a 9 × 5 × 3-inch loaf pan.

In a large bowl, sift together the flour, baking soda, and salt. In a separate bowl, mix the oil, sugar, banana, eggs, and milk. Add the wet ingredients to the dry ingredients. Stir in the nuts.

Bake for about an hour, until the bread springs back when you lightly touch the top of the loaf. Cool in the pan, then wrap the loaf tightly to store MAKES **1** LOAF

slob smarts Place your bananas in a paper bag to ripen for a day or two if they are too green. To ripen them even faster, try placing an apple or a tomato in the bag along with the bananas.

bran, nut, and raisin bread 

THE FIRST AIRLINE FOOD was served aboard a passenger plane on April 8, 1930. It was a joint venture between the Kellogg Company (which provided the food) and the Ford Motor Company (which provided the Tri-motor Cub plane). During the flight, Mary I. Barber, the home economics director of Kellogg, served lunch to fifteen presidents of a Detroit women's organization. They were served a bread made with bran cereal, nuts, and raisins. There is no record of how many passengers joined the "mile-high club" that day. (Source: *The Best Recipes from the Backs of Boxes, Bottles, Cans and Jars* by Ceil Dyer.)

- 1½ cups all-purpose flour
- 1 tablespoon baking powder
- 1 teaspoon salt
- 1½ cups Kellogg's All-Bran cereal
- ⅓ cup firmly packed brown sugar
- ¾ cup milk
- ⅓ cup molasses
- ¾ cup walnut pieces
- ¾ cup raisins

Preheat the oven to 350°F. Grease a 9 × 5 × 3-inch loaf pan.

In a mixing bowl, sift together the flour, baking powder, and salt and set aside.

In a mixing bowl, blend together the cereal, brown sugar, milk, 3/4 cup of water, and the molasses. Stir in the flour mixture and add the walnuts and raisins.

Spread the batter in the loaf pan and bake for 1 hour, or until a toothpick or cake tester inserted near the center of the bread comes out clean. Cool on a wire rack. MAKES 1 LOAF

crumpets

I USUALLY AVOID BAKING YEAST BREADS the way Jodie Foster avoids love scenes. One morning, however, in a frenzy of domestic enthusiasm, I made these crumpets. I adapted the recipe from a very reliable source, *A Window Over the Sink,* by my favorite cookbook author and best friend in the kitchen, Peg Bracken. She has never steered me wrong, bless her. Most crumpet recipes are harder than Chinese arithmetic, but there is simplicity in her instruction.

The original recipe called for an unusual piece of equipment called a "crumpet ring." Since I don't keep crumpet rings, or butter churns, or a meat grinder in my arsenal of cooking equipment, I improvised. Locating some biscuit cutters in my junk drawer and a few empty tuna cans from the recycling bin, I went about making crumpets with great success. Just use your head and adjust the griddle cooking times, as the smaller ones cook more quickly. I was very happy with the resultant crumpets, as was my family. Now my father requests them, and I have dug myself into a pit.

1 tablespoon dry yeast
1 cup milk, heated
2 tablespoons sugar
1 teaspoon salt
1 egg
2 cups all-purpose flour
3 tablespoons butter for greasing the skillet
Butter, for serving (see recipe on page 200)
Jam, for serving

In a small bowl, sprinkle the yeast over 1/2 cup of warm water. Pour the heated milk into a large bowl and add the sugar and salt.

Stir the yeast mixture and add it to the milk mixture along with the egg and flour. Beat thoroughly, then cover and let the batter rise for 30 minutes. Beat again for 4 minutes, then let the batter rise for another 30 minutes.

Grease the griddle and the crumpet rings or can rings. Place the greased rings on the greased skillet. Fill the rings with batter, and cook for 8 to 10 minutes on each side. The crumpets will develop a golden crust and will rise gently in the center.

Serve with butter and jam. MAKES ABOUT **8** CRUMPETS

slob smarts You burn more calories sleeping than you do watching TV. But what if you fall asleep watching TV? The average person resting comfortably for 24 hours or for 48 30-minute back-to-back episodes of *I Love Lucy* will burn off about 1,700 calories.

butter

IF YOU ARE BAKING BREAD, why not take a crack at making fresh butter as well? You don't need a churn; an electric mixer will work just fine. It's a virtuous way to kill some time if you are cooped up in the house some rainy afternoon.

• • •

Pour 2 cups of heavy cream into a deep bowl, and add 1 teaspoon of salt. Beat the cream at medium speed until it looks like whipped cream. Keep beating past the whipped cream stage, until it looks curdled and separates into butter and whey. (Now you have a visual reference for what Miss Muffet was ingesting.) This will take between 5 and 8 minutes, depending on the mixer speed.

Scoop up the butter in your hands and squeeze out the whey. Transfer the butter to a clean bowl, cover with plastic wrap, and store in the refrigerator, where it will last for about a month.

MAKES ABOUT **1** CUP

slob smarts Saint Brigit of Ireland was known for her generosity, which enabled her to feed strangers with her miraculous supply of endless butter. (Source: *Much Depends on Dinner,* by Margaret Visser, 1986.)

The hardness of the butter is proportional to the softness of the bread.

—STEVEN WRIGHT

peach raspberry butter

My husband and I call the small orchard at our farm "the Fruit Cup." We have apple, peach, and pear trees, as well as raspberries, blueberries, and wild strawberries. Every year in late summer, my best friend, Lynn, and I make peach butter. Last year we made a huge batch, using seventy pounds of peaches in a pot large enough to poach a missionary.

Fruit butters are easier to make than jams or jellies, which need pectin to gel and have to be packed in sterilized jars and boiled to "can" them. Fruit butters are more rustic, like a fruit reduction. They must be refrigerated and will stay fresh there for about a month.

If you don't have an orchard out on the fire escape this recipe produces a more reasonable yield.

• • •

In a large saucepan, place 2 cups chopped peaches, 1 cup raspberries, 1/3 cup sugar, and 2 tablespoons fruit-flavored brandy, Grand Marnier, Chambord, or vanilla vodka, for a kick and enhanced flavor. (It's fine to leave it out if you prefer.) Bring to a boil, then reduce the heat to medium-high and cook, stirring occasionally for about 15 minutes. The mixture will thicken to spreadable consistency.

Cool the peach butter to room temperature, then transfer into a plastic food storage containers or clean recycled glass jars.

MAKES **3** 4-OUNCE JARS

slob smarts In the nineteenth century, golfers were accompanied by a caddy and another assistant called a jam boy. The idea was that the jam boy acted like a bug magnet so the golfer would not be bothered by flying insects. Next time your kid whines about unloading the dishwasher, tell him he's lucky he's not a jam boy and then tell him the story. That should straighten him out.

The trouble with resisting temptation is that you may not got another chance.

—EDWIN CHAPIN

sweet talk

for those who consider

a cupcake in each hand

a balanced diet

EVERYTHING in moderation, including moderation. So if you go off on a cookie binge every once in a while, you are on the right track. When I was a kid, my sister Kate and I spent hours baking miniature culinary oddities beneath a 100-watt light bulb. **Our Easy-Bake oven ignited my domestic curiosity.** Now, many years later, I have put away my childish things. I no longer have the patience to bake one cookie at a time. At ten minutes per cookie, a mere half dozen would take more than an hour. **Yet the idea of baking in small quantities still appeals to my potent sense of modern immaturity.**

With that thought in my mind, I bought a toaster oven, the grown-up's equivalent of that fondly remembered Easy-Bake. The toaster oven is indispensable. When I'm cooking for a crowd, I use it to bake side dishes. But the real genius of this appliance comes at dessert time.

When it's just me and a friend or two, I use it to bake tiny cakes and small batches of cookies and brownies. If you don't have tiny-size cookware, **I have had great success baking cakes in coffee tins and soup cans.** I discovered this one day when, in a fit of overzealousness, I was rinsing out some cans to place in the recycling bin. I thought that if I greased and floured the interiors, I could bake an individual cake for everyone coming for dinner that night. It worked beautifully; and **if you are not having fun in the kitchen, what are you having?**

To bake a cake in a coffee or a soup can, wash out an empty can that was opened on one end. Grease and flour the inside of the can, and fill it one-quarter to one-half full with your favorite cake-mix batter. Bake according to the package directions for cupcakes. Test for doneness by inserting a toothpick into the center. If it comes out clean, then the cake is done. Cool for 5 minutes in the can, then invert, remove from the can, and continue to cool on a cooling rack. Frost as usual and serve with a flourish.

ice cream slob smarts

MORE ICE CREAM is consumed in America than anywhere else in the world, with the average person eating 15 to 20 quarts each year. Here are some interesting tidbits of information and quotes about this creamy confection.

- Ice cream is thought to have first been made in Italy in the 1600s. Thomas Jefferson's cook had a recipe for ice cream and introduced it to Dolley Madison, who served it at her husband's second inaugural ball in 1812. Ingredients were beaten by hand and then shaken in a pot of ice and salt. The hand-cranked ice cream freezer was invented in 1846.

- The ice cream cone was a collaboration between two vendors at the 1904 St. Louis World's Fair. One guy was selling ice cream and another, Ernest A. Hamwi, a Syrian, was selling *zalabia*—a soft cookie. When the ice cream dude ran out of dishes, the *zalabia* salesman rolled one of his warm, pliable cookies into a cone. The cone was filled with ice cream—and was an instant success. Mr. Hamwi founded Western Cone Company and became very rich.

- According to the *Oxford Modern English Dictionary,* caloric value is the amount of heat produced by a specified quantity of food. Since calories are measured by heat, can ice cream and frozen margaritas be excluded from calorie counting?

- An ice cream headache is triggered by the sudden change in temperature that occurs in your mouth when you eat something cold. The cold ice cream touches the roof of your mouth and initiates a nerve reaction that swells the blood vessels in your head. The nerve center in the roof of your mouth overreacts to the cold temperatures of the ice cream and tries to heat your brain. This sensation can last for thirty to sixty seconds.

Ice-cream is exquisite. What a pity it isn't illegal.

—Voltaire

kick-the-can ice cream 

A RECIPE REQUIRING DUCT TAPE? In my book, it sounds like fun. Since it *is* my book, I will tell you that this is my favorite. I usually pull this recipe out of my bag of tricks when I have kids visiting, and it is always a crowd pleaser. The hardware store will sell you clean, new gallon and quart paint cans; scrub them out before you use them.

- 1 cup milk
- 1 cup heavy cream
- ½ cup sugar
- 1 tablespoon vanilla extract

EQUIPMENT

- Clean 1-pound coffee can with plastic lid
- Clean 3-pound coffee can with plastic lid
- Duct tape
- Rock salt
- Crushed ice

Pour the milk, cream, sugar, and vanilla into the 1-pound can. Place the lid on the small can, and tape securely all around with duct tape.

Shove an inch or so of ice into the large can and cover it with rock salt. Place the small can into the large can, and continue to add layers of ice and salt up and over the small can. Tape on the top of the large can securely with more duct tape.

Find some kids and get them to kick the can around the backyard for about 15 minutes. It will make a racket, and it will keep the kids busy for an entire quarter of an hour.

Open the large can and drain out the water. Peek into the small can to see if the ice cream has frozen. If it's still kind of soupy, add more ice to the large can and kick it around for another 5 minutes (or put the small can in the freezer until it sets). MAKES **4** ½-CUP SERVINGS

VARIATION Try using resealable plastic bags. Fill a gallon bag with ice and add rock salt.

Pour the milk, cream, sugar, and vanilla into a pint bag. Seal the pint bag and place it in the ice-filled gallon bag. Seal and shake the bag for 8 minutes, or until the ice cream mixture freezes

ice cream balls 

When people ask, "Did you make these?" you can reply, "I made them *better.*" These ice cream bonbons are a snap to make and look as if they took more effort than scooping and dunking. I keep a stash in the freezer.

- 1 quart vanilla or coffee ice cream
- 1 cup finely chopped nuts
- 1 cup chocolate sauce

Scoop the ice cream into small balls using a melon baller. Roll the balls in the chopped nuts. Freeze until firm. Dip the ice cream balls into chocolate sauce and refreeze them for at least 1 hour.

SERVES **6** TO **8**

Cleaning the house while you still have kids living at home is like shoveling the walk while it is still snowing.

—PHYLLIS DILLER

jam tarts

I LIKE TO USE lemon curd in this recipe, but "Curd Tarts" doesn't have as nice a ring to it, does it?

- 1/2 cup (1 stick) unsalted butter, softened
- 5 ounces cream cheese, softened
- 1 cup flour
- 1 cup fruit jam or lemon curd

Preheat the oven to 450°F. Grease a baking sheet with butter.

In a mixing bowl, combine the butter, cream cheese, and flour to make a soft dough (using your fingers is the easiest way).

Pinch off a walnut-sized ball of dough and press it into a flat circle on a lightly floured surface. Place a teaspoon of jam on the dough disk, fold it into a half-moon shape, and crimp the edges with a floured fork to seal the tart. Repeat with the remaining dough and jam.

Place the tarts on the baking sheet and bake for 10 to 15 minutes, until lightly browned. MAKES ABOUT 18 TARTS.

peanut butter cookies 

THESE ARE THE EASIEST COOKIES in the world to make. In fact, I brought them to my meetings with publishers to get a deal for this book. Well, you are reading it, so I know they were a hit. This is a great recipe to have up your oven mitt, perfect for those mornings when your child tells you there is a school bake sale and he needs to take in a plate of cookies in 20 minutes.

Oscar winners Michael Moore and Kathleen Glynn, who wrote, produced, and directed my favorite movie of all time, *Roger and Me,* partially financed their film with bake sales. They would have made a fortune with these cookies.

1 cup chunky or smooth peanut butter
1 cup sugar (try dark brown, white, or light brown; they all work and taste great)
1 egg

Preheat the oven to 350°F.

Mix the peanut butter, sugar, and egg together with a fork. The dough will be sticky. Roll into 1-inch balls and place on an ungreased cookie sheet. Press down the balls with a fork to make the traditional international symbol for peanut butter cookies.

Bake for 8 to 10 minutes. Allow the cookies to cool on the baking sheet for 10 minutes, until they are set. Then transfer to a wire rack or right into your pie hole. MAKES ABOUT **24** COOKIES

slob smarts If you pinch the cookies in the middle before baking, they will resemble peanuts.

toffee-covered graham crackers 

GRAHAM CRACKERS were named for the nineteenth-century champion of whole-meal wheat (graham) flour and vegetarianism in general, Sylvester Graham, who invented them in 1829. A Presbyterian minister and a health nut, Graham believed that physical lust was harmful to the body and could cause insanity. He felt a strict vegetarian diet would aid in suppressing carnal urges. These rich cookies have the opposite effect.

12 graham crackers
3/4 cup (1 1/2 sticks) butter
1/2 cup brown sugar, packed
1/8 teaspoon salt
1 1/2 cups chocolate chips
1 cup chopped nuts

Preheat the oven to 350°F.

Line a large baking sheet with aluminum foil (if you don't, the toffee will stick to the pan and make a mess). Arrange the graham crackers on the foil.

In a saucepan, melt the butter over medium heat. Add the brown sugar and salt, and whisk together until smooth. Pour the melted butter-sugar mixture evenly over the graham crackers and bake for 10 minutes.

Remove the pan from the oven, and sprinkle the chocolate chips over the top of the crackers. Top with the chopped nuts. Return the pan to the oven until the chocolate melts, about 7 minutes.

Let cool and break up the crackers. Store in a covered container.

MAKES ABOUT **12** CRACKERS

slob smarts Use only stick butter in recipes. Whipped butter in a tub has air incorporated into it, and it will screw up your measurements.

jane ford's flash-in-a-pan cookies 

JANE FORD is one of the best cooks I've ever met. She cooked for the priests at our parish, Our Lady of Mercy. Her charm, ingenuity, and great taste are legend, and I am proud to share her recipe in my book —especially since it's such a great shortcut.

- **1 package cake mix (any flavor)**
- **2 eggs**
- **1/2 cup vegetable oil**

Preheat the oven to 350°F.

In a large bowl, mix the cake mix, eggs, and oil until any lumps are incorporated into the dough. The dough will be stiff and sticky.

Drop the batter by spoonfuls onto an ungreased cookie sheet, about 2 inches apart. Bake for 10 minutes, or until set. MAKES ABOUT **24** COOKIES

VARIATION I can make batter for chocolate chip cookies or I can add chips to Jane Ford's recipe and no one knows the difference. Stir in 2 cups of chocolate chips to the recipe above.

slob smarts When rolling cookie dough, dust the rolling pin with powdered sugar instead of flour. Too much flour can make cookies tough. Too much sugar? There's no such thing.

stomachache in a can 

(rum balls)

MY FRIEND PEG and I make these at Christmas time and give them out in decorated coffee cans. My former boss at MTV, Dave Ladik, named them "stomachache in a can" because he ate too many.

- **2 cups graham cracker crumbs**
- **2 tablespoons cocoa powder**
- **1 cup powdered sugar, plus more for rolling the balls**
- **2 tablespoons honey**
- **1/4 cup dark rum**

In a mixing bowl, combine the graham cracker crumbs, cocoa, and powdered sugar. Stir in the honey and rum.

Roll the mixture into 1-inch balls, then roll the balls in powdered sugar.

Store in a covered container such as a coffee can to ripen and enhance the rum flavor. They stay fresh for about 1 month.

MAKES ABOUT **24** RUM BALLS

> When we lose twenty pounds . . . we may be losing the twenty best pounds we have! We may be losing the pounds that contain our genius, our humanity, our love and honesty.
>
> —WOODY ALLEN

sticky toffee pie

THIS PIE IS SO ADDICTIVE it should be served by prescription. It is so sweet it would make Garrison Keillor gag. In other words, this pie will rock your world.

¼ cup (½ stick) butter, melted
2 cups dark brown sugar, firmly packed
3 eggs
1 9-inch pie crust, unbaked

Preheat the oven to 350°F.

In a medium bowl, stir together the melted butter and the sugar until blended. Mix in the eggs and beat with a fork for about 30 seconds.

Pour into the pie crust and bake for 30 to 35 minutes, until the pie is set and the center is slightly puffed up. SERVES **6** TO **8**

slob smarts Buy an assortment of small pastries and serve them on a platter—cannoli, cupcakes, dipped strawberries, and small tarts. Create a dessert centerpiece with a huge pile of penny candy, miniature candy bars, candy necklaces, and wax lips.

As for butter versus margarine, I trust cows more than chemists.

—JOAN GUSSOW

candace bushnell's key lime pie 

SOME PEOPLE MAY ACCEPT a bowl of fresh fruit as dessert, but they don't come to eat at my house. Practically everyone prefers pie and ice cream. My friend Candace makes this, and she was sweet enough to share the recipe with all of us.

If you are going to use bottled lime juice, use only Key lime juice. Better yet, buy regular limes and juice them. Using the juice from a plastic lime is not encouraged. This is an easy recipe; don't punk out.

FOR THE FILLING

- 1 cup Key lime juice, fresh or bottled
- 2 14-ounce cans sweetened condensed milk
- 2 eggs
- 2 egg whites

9-inch graham cracker crust

Whipped cream, for garnish
Zest of 1 lime, for garnish

Preheat the oven to 350°F.

In a bowl, whisk together the filling ingredients until blended and creamy. Pour into the crust.

Bake for 30 to 35 minutes, or until firm. Cool to room temperature, then refrigerate. Serve with whipped cream and garnish with lime zest. SERVES **6**

slob smarts If a recipe calls for egg yolks only, reserve the whites. They freeze very well for meringues, soufflés, and frosting. Just beat in a few teaspoons of sugar before freezing, and label the container so you know how many you have.

Condensed milk is wonderful. I don't see how they can get a cow to sit down on those little cans.

—FRED ALLEN

fudge pie

SOMETIMES AN INNER VOICE tells me to eat right. When it does, I shut it up with a nice big slice of fudge pie.

- ½ cup (1 stick) butter, melted
- ¼ cup cocoa powder
- 1 cup sugar
- ½ cup flour
- 2 eggs
- 1 tablespoon vanilla extract
- Pinch of salt
- Whipped cream, for garnish
- Fresh berries, for garnish

On chocolate: "It flatters you for a while, it warms you for an instant; then all of a sudden, it kindles a mortal fever in you."

—MARIE, MARQUISE DE SÉVIGNÉ, SEVENTEENTH CENTURY

Preheat the oven to 325°F.

In a medium bowl, stir together the butter, cocoa, sugar, flour, eggs, vanilla, and salt.

Pour the batter into a greased pie pan and bake for 20 minutes. Serve with whipped cream and berries. SERVES **6**

slob smarts Chocolate contains phenylethylamine (PEA), a natural substance that is reputed to stimulate the same reaction in the body as falling in love.

Forget about calories—everything makes thin people thinner, and fat people fatter.

—MIGNON MCLAUGHLIN, *THE SECOND NEUROTIC'S NOTEBOOK,* 1966

rustic tarts

A QUAINT, EVOCATIVE NAME for the marriage of refrigerated dough and canned pie filling, yet the sum of these two commercial ingredients is a homemade-looking tart. Well, they *are* homemade—you emptied that can of fruit filling into the pie crust, didn't you?

- 2 refrigerated pie crusts (not the kind that come in a pie tin)
- 1 15-ounce can fruit pie filling (cherry, blueberry, apple)
- 1 egg
- Powdered sugar, for dusting

Preheat the oven to 350°F.

Unfold two sheets of pie dough on a greased baking sheet. Spoon pie filling onto half of each of the dough sheets and fold the other half over the filling. Press the seam with a fork. It will look like a large empanada.

Break the egg in a cup, mix with 1 tablespoon water, and beat with a fork. Paint the egg wash over the top of the tarts and bake for 20 to 25 minutes. Cool on the baking sheet. Dust the top with powdered sugar before serving. MAKES **2** TARTS

O, blackberry tart, with berries as big as your thumb,
purple and black, and thick with juice, and a crust to
endear them that will go to cream in your mouth,
and both passing down with such a taste that will
make you close your eyes and wish you might
live forever in the wideness of that rich moment.

—RICHARD LLEWELLYN

cookie crumb crust for pies 

CRUMB CRUSTS ARE VERY GOOD, and very easy to make. If you want to make pie pastry from scratch, I'm sorry, I can't help you. Go to your big, fat comprehensive cookbook. I think these crumb crusts are great, and after all, you are making dessert, not entering a bake-off. A crumb crust does not label you deficient in homemaking skills; it shows that you are a smart cookie. To crumble graham crackers, vanilla wafers, or chocolate wafers, toss in a heavy-duty resealable plastic bag and crush with a rolling pin or a chilled bottle of wine.

You can use about 15 whole crushed graham crackers, or the equivalent in shortbread or chocolate sandwich cookies, as you prefer. If you remember, skimp a bit on the crust and save a few tablespoons of the crumb mixture to sprinkle on top of the filling.

1½ cups cookie crumbs
4 tablespoons sugar
¼ cup (½ stick) butter, melted

In the pie pan you will be serving from, mix together the crumbs and sugar, then add the butter. Mix until all the crumbs are moistened. Press evenly onto the bottom and sides of the pan with your fingertips. Then either chill the crust for 30 minutes before you fill it and bake it, or bake it empty at 350°F. for 15 minutes if you will be using an uncooked filling. LINES ONE **9**-INCH PIE PAN

Promises and pie crusts are meant to be broken.

—JONATHAN SWIFT

fruit crumble

MILK THE UDDERS OF NOSTALGIA with this recipe. Driving through the neck-snappingly beautiful state of Maine, my husband and I entertain ourselves by playing a game in which we invent imaginary "Maine-sounding" town names, like Squabnocket, East Chubby Neck, Stickasockinit, Upperbelly Port. . . . You get the idea.

There actually is a town called Eggomoggin, and after purchasing a few pints of wild Maine blueberries there, I made this.

- ¾ cup brown sugar, packed
- 1 cup old-fashioned oatmeal (not instant)
- ½ cup all-purpose flour
- 4 cups fruit of your choice, such as raspberries, blueberries, sliced peaches, or strawberries, or a mixture
- Sugar to taste
- 3 tablespoons butter, cut into small bits

Preheat the oven to 350°F.

In a medium bowl, mix together the brown sugar, oatmeal, and flour.

Place the fruit in a pie pan or ovenproof dish. Sprinkle with sugar if the fruit is too tart. Sprinkle the crumble topping over the fruit, and scatter the bits of butter over the topping. Bake for 40 minutes, or until the top is browned and the fruit is bubbling. SERVES **4** TO **6**

slob smarts Just so you know, a fruit crisp or crumble is fruit topped with a layer of flour, sugar, and butter that bakes into a crispy topping. Cobbler is fruit baked with a biscuit topping.

baked alaska pie

TRADITIONAL BAKED ALASKA is a sponge cake layered with ice cream, then topped with egg-white meringue. I prefer pie over cake, and this adapted recipe is an improvement over the original. You can use a purchased graham cracker crust if you insist.

- **1 quart ice cream (any flavor), softened**
- **1 Cookie Crumb Crust (page 217), made with graham cracker crumbs**
- **3 egg whites**
- **1 cup marshmallow creme**

Preheat the oven to 500°F.

Spoon the softened ice cream into the crust and put in the freezer to chill.

Beat the egg whites with an electric mixer until soft peaks form. Gradually incorporate the marshmallow creme into the eggs, beating until stiff peaks form. Spread over the frozen ice cream pie, covering it completely.

Slide the pie into the oven for 3 minutes, or until the meringue toasts and is lightly browned. Serve immediately to your wildly impressed guests. SERVES **6**

slob smarts Baked Alaska originated in 1876 at the legendary Delmonico's Restaurant, located in New York City. It was created in honor of the newly acquired territory of Alaska.

shut-your-pie-hole pie 

I HEARD THIS RECIPE discussed on a radio call-in show. All the ingredients are poured in a blender and that is as laborious as it gets. During the baking process, the ingredients sort themselves out: The baking mix settles with the coconut to make a crust and the eggs and milk make a baked custard filling. I couldn't believe how easy this is to make; it's actually as easy as pie. I whip this up and serve it to family and dinner guests, and even bring it as a hostess gift.

- 2 cups milk
- 3/4 cup sugar
- 1/2 cup biscuit baking mix (such as Bisquick)
- 1/4 cup (1/2 stick) butter, at room temperature and cut into dice-size chunks (see headnote)
- 4 eggs
- 1 1/2 teaspoons vanilla extract
- 1 cup flaked coconut

Preheat the oven to 350°F. Grease a deep 9-inch pie pan and set the pan on a baking sheet, to prevent spills.

Place all the ingredients in a blender, cover, and blend for 20 seconds. Pour into the prepared pie plate. (If you only have a shallow pie pan, pour the extra 1/2 cup of filling into an ovenproof bowl or custard cup to make a small serving to share.) Bake for 50 minutes, or until puffed and golden brown. SERVES **6**

slob smarts Room temperature is the temperature of any room. My tiny kitchen in New York City is hotter than the subway in August. My drafty ancient farmhouse kitchen has me shivering like an overbred poodle. Room-temperature cream cheese or butter should be softened; it doesn't really matter the temperature of the room. Special note to my arctic readers: You're screwed.

crepes redhead

A MEAN OLD GOAT of a woman taught me this recipe. The crepes are great, but the nameless sourpuss is the most horrible woman on the face of the planet. So, I took Old Ugly's recipe and changed the name, using the term of endearment I use for my mom, Carol "Redhead" Duffy, the most amazing, beautiful, kind, talented, and loving person in the world.

We eat these with jam or maple syrup, or fill them with fresh berries.

- 3 eggs
- ½ cup milk
- 2 tablespoons butter, melted
- ½ cup flour
- 1 teaspoon sugar
- Pinch of salt

Combine all the ingredients in a blender and blend. Refrigerate for at least 1 hour, or overnight.

Lightly butter two 6-inch crepe pans. Pour 1/8 cup batter into a pan and tilt and swirl the butter to coat the pan evenly. Cook until the edges darken slightly and bubble. Flip with a spatula and cook on the other side. Gently remove from the pan and place on a plate lined with wax paper.

Cover with plastic wrap and store in refrigerator. MAKES ABOUT **15** CREPES

I'm in shape. Round is a shape . . . isn't it?

—ANONYMOUS

cheesecake codependency 

CHEESECAKE CODEPENDENCY is when you order a slice, and your dining partner eats half of it. I do not encourage deceptive dessert behavior, and I do encourage everyone to order his or her own damn cheesecake. If you are feeling particularly benevolent, you could even bake a cheesecake for your fork-wielding, dessert-snatching friend.

- 1 pound cream cheese, at room temperature
- 2 eggs at room temperature, lightly beaten
- ⅔ cup plus 3 tablespoons sugar
- 1 vanilla bean
- 1 Cookie Crumb Crust (see page 217), made with ¼ teaspoon cinnamon in a 9-inch springform pan
- 1½ cups sour cream

Preheat the oven to 350°F. and place a baking sheet on the center rack.

With an electric mixer, beat the cream cheese until creamy and fluffy. Add the eggs, ⅔ cup sugar, and the seeds from the vanilla bean (split it lengthwise and scrape seeds into the batter), and mix until very smooth. Scrape the bowl with a spatula to break up any lumps.

Pour the mixture into the crust, and place on the baking sheet. Bake for 25 minutes.

Meanwhile, in a bowl, blend the sour cream with the remaining 3 tablespoons of sugar. After 25 minutes, remove the cheesecake from the oven and raise the heat to 450°F. Gently spoon the sour cream mixture on top of the hot cheesecake, and spread it evenly. Return the cake to the oven, and bake for 7 minutes. Cool on a wire rack until ready to serve. SERVES **6**

eggs on a raft

MY FRIEND JON SADLIER, a naughty English playboy, is a cheeky monkey in the kitchen. His signature dish is chicken roulette—chicken salad with a bone mixed in. Whoever chokes on the bone wins. I won't bother to share that recipe, as I prefer my poultry without danger and my parties without drama or visits to the emergency room.

He does make a sly dessert that always gets a laugh first, and a rave second. This is ridiculously easy and memorable. You can get away with serving it to guests because it will crack them up.

- 1 ¾-inch slice of store-bought pound cake per person (or make your own from the recipe on page 226)
- 1 canned peach half, drained, per person
- Whipped cream, preferably from an aerosol spray can

Put a peach half on top of each slice of pound cake and squirt whipped cream around the peach, so it looks like a fried egg on toast. Serve with a straight face

The first of all considerations is that our food should be fun as well as fuel.

—ANDRE SIMPSON

sweetie-pie fries 

Bob Blumer, the Surreal Gourmet, has a lively and artistic sense of fun in the kitchen. He is always monkeying around with inventive ways to serve and entertain his dinner guests. One of my favorites is cake with raspberry sauce, sliced and served to resemble a plate of French fries with ketchup. He slices store-bought pound cake into strips the size of French fries, then toasts them in a 350°F. oven for 10 minutes, so they turn a legit golden color.

I would just pile them on a plate, but Bob makes cardboard containers to look like fast-food French fry cartons. He makes a raspberry sauce by simmering raspberries with sugar until the mixture reduces slightly and thickens to the consistency of ketchup. Then he presses it through a sieve to remove the seeds and pours it into a red condiment container.

I would just heat up a few tablespoons of raspberry jam, thin it with a splash of orange juice, and skip the sieve and squeeze bottle. I would toss the pound cake on a plate with a puddle of sauce. That's why Bob wrote *The Surreal Gourmet* and I wrote *A Slob in the Kitchen.*

slob smarts White sugar is essentially pure sucrose, derived from sugarcane or sugar beets. Brown sugar is white sugar with molasses syrup added to it (and Mick Jagger's preference).

The older you get the tougher it is to lose weight because by then you and your fat are really good friends.

—ANONYMOUS

marshmallow cake 

THE MARSHMALLOWS FLOAT to the top of this cake during the cooking process, creating a gooey frosting. It is easier than making s'mores, and it tastes even better.

1 bag marshmallows
1 package chocolate cake mix

Preheat the oven to 350°F., or whatever is called for on the package of cake mix.

Grease a 9 × 13-inch Pyrex baking dish.

Slice the marshmallows in half and arrange in the baking dish. Make the cake according to the package instructions. Pour the batter over the cut marshmallows and bake as directed. SERVES **12**

slob smarts If you're packing cupcakes for a picnic, slice them in half and frost the middles, then reassemble them. They will travel better.

PIPING HOT PEEPS

If you put a marshmallow chick (the kind you find in an Easter basket) in the microwave for 15 seconds, the little yellow chick will inflate to the size of a full-grown hen.

pound cake

POUND CAKE KEEPS WELL for several days, wrapped in plastic film. It also freezes beautifully. After you make it a few times, you can doctor up the batter with the juice and zest of a lemon. You can make a lemon glaze or a fruit jam sauce. You can top it with fresh fruit, but practically everyone prefers chocolate sauce. So now you know why they call it pound cake, right?

1 pound (4 sticks) butter, softened
1 pound (about 2⅓ cups) sugar
1 pound (8 to 10 large) eggs
1 tablespoon plus 1 teaspoon vanilla extract
1 teaspoon salt
1 pound (about 4 cups) flour

Preheat the oven to 350°F. Grease and flour two 9 × 5 × 3-inch loaf pans.

In a large bowl, with an electric mixer or a wooden spoon, beat the butter and sugar together until fluffy. Beat in the eggs, one at a time. Beat in the vanilla and salt. Add the flour, 1 cup at a time, beating well until the flour is incorporated and the batter is smooth.

Pour the batter into the prepared loaf pans and bake in the center of the oven for about 1 hour. The cake is done when the top is golden and cracked.

Cool in the pans for 5 minutes, then turn the cakes out of the pans onto racks to cool completely. MAKES **2** CAKES

slob smarts When you're adding dry ingredients like flour to batter in your mixer bowl, toss a clean dish towel over the mixer to keep batter from splashing all over the kitchen.

don't ask, don't tell cake 

IN MY NEIGHBORHOOD there are bakeries that will create a Barbie-doll cake. Which inspired this, my tribute to the troops.

- **1 package cake mix (any flavor)**
- **1 G.I. Joe doll**
- **1 can prepared icing**
- **1 cocktail pick decorated with an American flag**

Preheat the oven to 350°F. Grease a 12-cup Bundt cake pan.

Prepare the cake-mix batter as directed and pour into the pan. Bake according to the directions on the package.

After the cake cools, invert it from the pan.

Put the G.I. Joe in the center hole of the cake and decorate the cake with icing. Place the cocktail-pick flag in G.I. Joe's kung-fu-grip hand.

SERVES **12** TO **16**

slob smarts Home-baked cakes, even those made from a mix, have a certain charm if you simply frost them with icing and then arrange small plastic toys on top. Buy a cheap pack of farm animals and turn a plain birthday cake into an "Old Goat Cake."

I transformed a box of yellow cake mix into a hula-girl cake and won over the birthday boy with my scrappy ingenuity.

cake slob smarts

EVERY YEAR on my friend Lynn's birthday we decorate her birthday cakes with a greeting like "Mazel Tov, Moishe" or "Bon Voyage, Mugsy." We pretend that we forgot her birthday and ask the bakery to write a Wisenheimer greeting, like "Congratulations on your release from prison." A few months ago I was working on a TV project with a crew of whiny crybaby producers. To liven up the shoot, I went to Rocco's pastry shop and bought a huge Italian cheesecake and had the baker write, "So, you want a piece of me?" on it. Sometimes, it is not what you say, but how you say it. If you have something interesting to discuss, try writing it on top of a cake. My friend Kim served an "I'm pregnant" cake to her astonished and delighted husband. (I won't surprise my assistant with a "You're Fired!" cake, though.)

You can make a homemade icing piping bag by filling a resealable plastic bag with icing or melted chocolate. Snip off a tiny corner of the bag and squeeze the icing out to write greetings or make decorations.

For children's parties, it seems like everyone bakes cupcakes in wafer ice cream cones. I like to bake cupcakes in cups. Lightly grease ovenproof teacups and fill them halfway. I like to frost the cupcakes and serve them in the cups, set on a saucer. You can pick up mismatched teacups at garage sales and discount stores. Make sure they are sturdy and ovenproof, like old restaurant china. Four teacup cakes in a box would make a thoughtful hostess gift.

one-a-day-daily-dose vitamin cake 

YOU KNOW HOW A SPOONFUL OF SUGAR is supposed to help the medicine go down? Well, don't you think chocolate cake would make medicine go down even more easily? The idea is to bake this cake and then place your vitamins (or birth-control pills, Viagra, or any other prescription pills) around the perimeter of the cake. This way rather than wondering "Hey, did I take my meds today?" you can say, "Hey, it's time to take my daily dose of chocolate vitamin cake." Even without, it's pretty tasty.

- 1 cup sugar
- 1½ cups flour
- ⅓ cup cocoa powder
- 1 teaspoon baking soda
- ½ teaspoon salt
- 2 teaspoons vanilla extract
- ½ cup vegetable oil
- 1 cup cold water
- 2 tablespoons vinegar
- Whipped cream or powdered sugar for garnish

Preheat the oven to 350°F.

In an 8-inch square or 9-inch round cake pan, combine all the ingredients except the vinegar and vitamins. Mix with a fork or whisk until blended. Add the vinegar and quickly stir to blend it into the batter.

Bake for 20 to 25 minutes, or until the center of the cake is slightly puffed.

Serve with whipped cream, or top with powdered sugar.

MAKES **1** CAKE

slob smarts You can also cover the top of a warm cake with chocolate-covered peppermint patties and let them all melt together to create a frosting.

raspberry upside-down cake 

EXPERIMENT WITH YOUR FAVORITE FRUITS and cake mixes. Blueberry and peach are lovely as well.

- 1 10-ounce bag frozen raspberries
- 1 package vanilla or yellow cake mix

Preheat the oven to 350°F. Grease and flour two 9-inch round cake pans. Pour an even amount of frozen berries into each pan.

Prepare the cake mix and pour the batter over the berries. Bake according to the package directions.

Let the cakes cool in the pans, then invert them onto serving plates.

MAKES **2** CAKES

slob smarts The upside-down food genre needs more recipes; use your imagination. Try an upside-down margarita at your next party: Have your guests lie flat and pour tequila, Triple Sec, and lime juice down their gullets. When they sit up, give them a lime to suck on.

Susan Caliendo runs a specialty decorated cookie business in New York City called Rolling Pin Productions. She creates artistic custom-made portrait cookies, and is the best in the business. To order her edible artwork, check out her website, www.rollingpinproductions.com

mud pie chocolate cake 

YOU PROBABLY HAVE MOST of these ingredients lying around your kitchen right now, so why don't you do something nice for someone and make this cake? Some people call this Crazy Cake. I'd call you crazy if you didn't try it at least once. This recipe does not call for eggs and became a hit during the Depression. The cake is leavened with the baking soda and vinegar.

- 1½ cups flour
- 3 tablespoons cocoa powder
- 1 teaspoon baking soda
- 1 cup sugar
- ½ teaspoon salt
- 5 tablespoons vegetable oil
- 1 tablespoon vinegar
- 1 teaspoon vanilla extract

Preheat the oven to 350°F. Grease a 9-inch square cake pan.

Sift the flour, cocoa, baking soda, sugar, and salt right into the greased pan.

Poke 3 holes in the dry mix and in one pour the oil, in the second pour the vinegar, and in the third pour the vanilla and 1 cup of water, and mix it all up.

Bake for 25 to 30 minutes, or until a cake tester inserted in the center comes out clean. MAKES **1** CAKE

slob smarts If you don't have a sifter, sift dry ingredients through a sieve.

whoopie pies

THESE COOKIES ARE CAKE SANDWICHES with icing in the middle. Since you are starting with devil's food cake mix, you might have enough time to embroider a whoopie cushion cover.

- 1 package devil's food cake mix

FILLING

- ½ cup (1 stick) butter, at room temperature
- 1¼ cups powdered sugar
- 2 cups marshmallow creme
- 1 tablespoon vanilla extract

Butter 2 baking sheets. Preheat the oven to 350°F. or to the temperature specified in the directions for the cake mix.

Prepare the cake mix batter as directed on the package. Spoon mounds of cake batter onto the prepared baking sheets, about ¼ cup per mound and about 2 inches apart. You should have 16 mounds.

Bake for 15 to 20 minutes, or until the tops puff up and spring back when touched. Transfer to a rack to cool.

Make the filling by beating the butter, powdered sugar, marshmallow creme, and vanilla with an electric mixer at medium speed until smooth, about 3 minutes. It will be sticky. Spread a generous amount of filling on the flat sides of 8 cakes and make each a sandwich with a second cake. MAKES **8** PIES

slob smarts Vanilla is the extract of fermented and dried pods of several species of orchids.

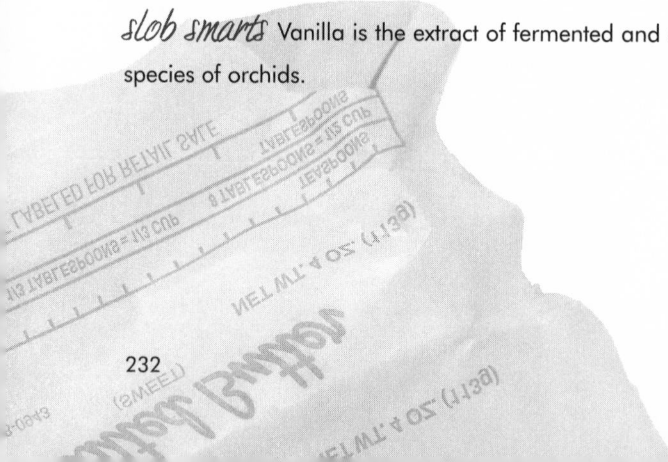

hot cocoa soufflé

THIS RECIPE ELEVATES EVERYDAY INGREDIENTS that you have on hand into something special. At our farm, we raise chickens, so we always have eggs. I can whip up this beginner soufflé in minutes, for teatime or anytime. It is remarkably easy and spectacularly delicious. I strenuously urge you to take a crack at making it.

1 cup plus 1 tablespoon sugar
3 tablespoons cocoa powder
5 egg whites
1 teaspoon vanilla extract
1/8 teaspoon salt
Fresh berries, for garnish (optional)
Whipped cream, for garnish (optional)

Preheat the oven to 350°F. Butter a 1 1/2-quart soufflé dish and then sprinkle in the tablespoon of sugar to coat the dish. Pour out any excess.

Sift together the remaining cup of sugar and the cocoa.

In a large bowl, beat the egg whites until stiff. Gradually add the sugar-cocoa mixture by the spoonful, and continue beating. Add the vanilla and salt. Beat until stiff peaks form. Pour the soufflé mixture into the prepared dish and then place the dish in a larger baking pan of warm water. Bake for 30 minutes, or until set in the center.

Serve immediately, on its own or with berries and whipped cream.

SERVES **6** TO **8**

slob smarts Egg whites whip better at room temperature. To speed up the process, place the whole eggs in a bowl of warm tap water for 5 minutes.

blueberry sauce

YOU CAN USE FRESH OR FROZEN BERRIES. Try raspberries or blackberries, too, and press the sauce through a sieve to remove the seeds if you are a type A personality.

- 2 cups blueberries
- 1 cup sugar

In a saucepan, combine the berries, sugar, and 2 tablespoons of water over medium heat. Bring to a simmer, stirring occasionally. Cook for 10 minutes, until the blueberries are tender. MAKES ABOUT **2** CUPS

caramel candy sauce 

- ½ pound soft caramel candies (about 20)
- ½ cup hot water

Place the caramels and water in the top of a double boiler. Heat over boiling water, stirring frequently, until the candies are melted and smooth. MAKES ABOUT **2** CUPS

whipped cream

EVERY TIME YOU OPEN A TUB of nondairy whipped dessert topping, an angel dies. To stop this senseless loss, grab a whisk, ½ pint of heavy cream, and 1 tablespoon of sugar. Whisk together for a few minutes, and save an angel. MAKES **1** CUP

crème fraîche

YOU CAN BUY IT, but it is ridiculously easy to make crème fraîche yourself. It's rich, thick, and tart. It is great with sweet berries.

1 cup heavy cream
1 cup sour cream

Whisk the ingredients together in a medium bowl and cover. Place the bowl in a warm spot, near the oven or on top of the refrigerator, for about 4 hours, until the mixture is thickened. Then refrigerate.
MAKES **2** CUPS

peanut butter sauce 

1 cup packed brown sugar
6 tablespoons milk
4 tablespoons light corn syrup
4 teaspoons butter
4 tablespoons peanut butter

In a saucepan, combine the brown sugar, milk, corn syrup, and butter. Cook and stir over medium heat until the sugar is melted and the mixture is smooth. Remove from the heat and stir in the peanut butter. MAKES **1 1/2** CUPS

hot fudge

IT'S BEEN SAID that one should be wary of any diet that discourages a liberal use of hot fudge sauce.

- 1 cup packed brown sugar
- 2/3 cup cocoa powder
- 1 teaspoon instant coffee
- 1/2 cup heavy cream
- 3 ounces semisweet chocolate chips
- 1 teaspoon vanilla
- 1/2 teaspoon cinnamon

In a saucepan, whisk together the sugar, cocoa, coffee, and cream. Bring to a simmer and cook for 3 minutes. Remove from the heat and stir in the chocolate chips until melted and smooth. Stir in the vanilla and cinnamon. MAKES 1 1/2 CUPS

slob smarts Aztec emperor Montezuma drank fifty golden goblets of hot chocolate every day. It was thick, dyed red, and flavored with chili peppers.

Always serve too much hot fudge sauce on hot fudge sundaes. It makes people overjoyed, and puts them in your debt.

—JUDITH OLNEY

creamy stovetop rice pudding 

A SHOP JUST OPENED in New York City called Rice To Riches. The only thing they sell is rice pudding, and they have twenty-one varieties, including Strawberry Floozy and Chocolate Cherry Crime-Scene.

- **4 cups milk**
- **½ cup regular, long-grain rice (uncooked)**
- **½ cup brown or white sugar**
- **1 tablespoon vanilla extract**
- **¼ teaspoon salt**
- **½ cup raisins or other dried fruit (optional)**
- **Freshly grated nutmeg, for garnish**

In a double boiler, or in a large metal bowl set snugly over a pot of simmering water, stir together the milk, rice, sugar, vanilla, and salt. Cover and cook over simmering water for 1½ to 2 hours, stirring frequently to separate the rice grains. The rice will be tender and creamy. Don't forget to check the water level in the bottom pot, adding water as needed to keep the pot full and at the simmering stage.

If adding dried fruit, stir it into the pudding after cooking. Serve garnished with a few sprinkles of nutmeg. SERVES **4**

No diet will remove all the fat from your body because the brain is entirely fat. Without a brain, you might look good, but all you could do is run for public office.

—GEORGE BERNARD SHAW

caramel apple shrunken heads 

YOU CAN DECORATE THESE APPLES to look like your in-laws, then bite their heads off (instead of their biting off yours).

1 14-ounce package of soft caramel candies
5 apples
5 wooden Popsicle sticks, or tongue depressors, or twigs from the backyard
Decorative candies, such as M&M's, marshmallows, or licorice

In a microwaveable bowl, combine the caramels and 2 tablespoons of water. Microwave on high for 2 minutes, stir, and return to the microwave for another 30 seconds. Repeat until the caramels are melted.

Insert the sticks into the apples, and dip into the melted caramel, covering completely. Place the apple-head sticks into empty soda cans so you don't have to hold the sticks when you decorate the faces with candy bits. MAKES **5**

Never work before breakfast; if you have to work before breakfast, eat your breakfast first.

—JOSH BILLINGS

wake and bake

sunny breakfast foods

that will perk your butt right up

THERE IS STRONG evidence that people who do not eat breakfast do not perform as well as people who do eat breakfast, and this is especially true for children. The morning meal supplies energy and nutrients your body needs after its overnight fast. In our society, where even the youngest members of the family leave the home in the morning, **breakfasting together not only refuels the body, it feeds the spirit.** When you share a morning meal with your kids, you reinforce the sense of parental protection and affection they need to feel secure and cared for if they are going to be separated from you for most of the day.

Further incentive: A study of 281 death-row inmates executed since 1986 revealed that only 7.5 percent chose breakfast as their final meal, and of all the females executed since 1970, not one chose breakfast. From this one could infer that **breakfast eaters are 93 percent**

less likely to be convicted of serious crimes than those who go without. If this information doesn't inspire you to make breakfast, I don't know what will.

With that in mind, I include here a selection of my favorite morning fare—**all so impressively easy to make you don't even need to be fully awake** to pull them off. Since we have a generous supply of eggs on our farm, I'm partial to this breakfast staple. They are so easy and versatile you have no excuse to resorting to boxed cereal for breakfast (much less dinner).

Love and eggs are best when they are fresh.

—RUSSIAN PROVERB

I am a light eater. When it gets light, I start eating.

—TOMMY JOHN

METHODS OF COOKING EGGS

Eggs provide sound nutritional value, and the speed and ease with which they can be prepared is a definite advantage. The best way to store eggs is in their carton in the refrigerator. Stored uncovered in the egg compartment in the refrigerator door, the eggs will absorb odors and lose moisture. Use the egg shelf in the refrigerator to store cologne, rolls of film, or your underwear, just like Marilyn Monroe did.

The difference between soft-boiled and hard-boiled eggs is how long the eggs stay in the water.

Soft-boiled eggs have a firm white and a runny yolk. (When he is sick, my husband requests two soft-cooked eggs chopped up in a mug, with salt and pepper, served with buttered toast cut into strips—not halves or triangles, strips. His appreciation is wildly disproportionate to the effort it takes to prepare. I thank my lovely mother-in-law for getting him hooked on such a simple meal.)

To make soft-boiled eggs using the cold-water method, place the eggs in a pan, cover with cold water, and slowly bring the water to a boil. Then cover, turn off the heat, and let the eggs stand for 3 to 5 minutes. While the eggs are standing, you can stare out the window and drain your coffee mug. Technically, you are now "cooking," so the person for whom you are making breakfast should go get the paper, feed the pets, or get the kids ready for school. It's only fair; you are busy in the kitchen.

> Eggs are small boys. If you overheat them or over beat them, they will turn on you, and no amount of future love will right the wrong.
>
> —ANONYMOUS

To make soft-boiled eggs using the hot-water method, get the water going in a pot, place the eggs into the boiling water, cover, and remove from the heat and let the eggs stand for 6 to 8 minutes.

Hard-boiled eggs have a firmly set white and yolk. If an egg is overcooked, a dark green line forms between the white and the yolk, caused when the sulfide in the white combines with the iron in the yolk. It is fine to eat, but unsightly, and can be avoided by proper cooking. Prepare according to either method above, allowing 10 to 12 minutes for the cold-water method or 6 to 8 minutes for the hot-water method. Drain and cover with cold water to make the shells easier to remove.

HARD-BOILED EGGS KARAOKE STYLE

A letter to the editor of the *London Daily Telegraph* suggested that if you boil an egg while singing all five verses and the chorus of the hymn "Onward Christian Soldiers," the egg will be cooked perfectly when you come to "amen."

My take on this method is to adapt it to my favorite classic rock anthem, Lynyyrd Skynyrd's "Freebird." Fill a saucepan with cold water and add eggs. Sing "Freebird" and play the air guitar solo while the eggs boil over high heat. At the end of the seven-minute song, your egg is cooked.

"free bird"

ALLEN COLLINS - RONNIE VAN ZANT

If I leave here tomorrow
Would you still remember me?
For I must be traveling on, now,
'Cause there's too many places I've got to see.
But, if I stayed here with you, girl,
Things just couldn't be the same.
'Cause I'm as free as a bird now,
And this bird you can not change.
Lord knows, I can't change.

Bye, bye, its been a sweet love.
Though this feeling I can't change.
But please don't take it badly,
'Cause Lord knows I'm to blame.
But, if I stayed here with you girl,
Things just couldn't be the same.
Cause I'm as free as a bird now,
And this bird you'll never change.
And this bird you can not change.
Lord knows, I can't change.
Lord help me, I can't change.

stuffed eggs

QUICKER THAN YOU CAN SAY "retro swing-dancing hep cat" you can make these old-school picnic and party snacks.

. . .

Halve peeled hard-boiled eggs lengthwise and poke out the yolks. Mash the yolks with a bit of mustard, mayonnaise, and the seasonings you prefer. Stuff the yolks back into the egg halves and refrigerate or serve.

slob smarts A fresh egg has a shell that is rough and chalky, an old egg has a shell that is smooth and shiny, and when something starts pecking its way out of the shell it is probably past its peak.

eggs in a nest

THE CHICKEN LAYS THE EGG in a nest and I collect it and make a nest out of toast. It's all part of the circle of life.

- **6 bread slices**
- **6 large eggs**

Preheat the oven to 350°F. Lightly grease a 6-cup muffin pan.

Press a slice of bread into each muffin cup and crack an egg into each bread cup. Bake for 15 to 20 minutes, until set. SERVES **6**

slob smarts If you are having a hectic week, knock off these two chores at once. While you are clearing the table from dinner, set it for breakfast.

coddled eggs

When my stomach alarm goes off, I silence it with coddled eggs. I eat eggs so often, I sometimes feel like Irwin Rose, the "Sausage and Egg Hermit," who ordered the same meal from his neighborhood deli three times a day for more than eight years. His strict diet was two fried eggs, sausage, rice pudding, and cheesecake. Mr. Rose, I regret to say, has since passed on.

Coddled eggs are similar to poached eggs but more delicate in texture. Make them in an egg coddler, a ceramic cup that looks like a custard cup with a lid.

Egg coddlers can be found in specialty houseware shops, and I have found fabulous vintage Royal Doulton china coddlers at online auctions for very reasonable prices.

• • •

Crack a raw egg into the buttered coddler, screw on the metal top, and place it in a pan of simmering water for 6 to 10 minutes, depending on how firm you like your eggs. Let the coddler stand in the water off the heat or keep the water simmering. You can add bits of bacon, smoked salmon, crumbled bits of cheese, or herbs and spices before you place the coddlers in the pot of water.

slob smarts To check the freshness of an egg, put it in a deep bowl of cold water. If it floats to the top, chuck it out; it is too old to use.

Ham and eggs—a day's work for a chicken; a lifetime commitment for a pig.

—ANONYMOUS

breakfast fruit smoothies 

THE TWO STATEMENTS about diet and nutrition that everyone should heed are (1) breakfast is the most important meal of the day and (2) the daily recommended requirement for fruits and vegetables is five a day.

Some days getting all five servings of fruits and vegetables into my system feels like a part-time job, so I made an appointment with a nutritionist to get some pointers. Oz Garcia is a bestselling author and a nutritionist with a client roster of busy New Yorkers. I asked for his number one tip for improving my diet, and he gave me this fruit smoothie recipe. It is very easy to whip up a batch, and it lets me squeeze three servings of fruit into breakfast. I use frozen berries, and I peel ripe bananas, break them in half, and keep them in a resealable plastic bag in the freezer.

½ cup milk, soy milk, or fruit juice
½ cup frozen berries
½ banana
2 tablespoons yogurt
Ice

Put everything in a blender and give it a whirl. SERVES **1**

> The first duty of the mistress after breakfast is to give her orders for the day, and she naturally begins with the cook. On entering the kitchen, invariably say, "Good morning, cook." (A courtesy much appreciated below stairs.)
>
> —ISABELLA BEETON, *EVERY-DAY COOKERY*, 1872

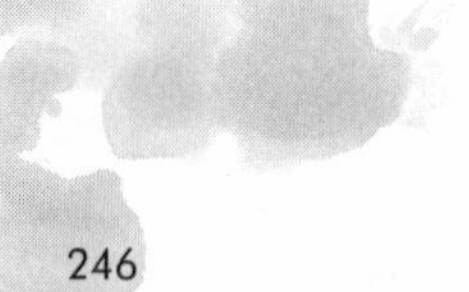

chips and fresh fruit salsa 

I ONCE READ that you are most likely to suffer a stroke or heart attack between eight and nine in the morning. Therefore, I propose that you stay in the feathers until ten A.M., and sleep safely through the danger hour. At ten o'clock, get up and make yourself a nice breakfast. If you are tired of eggs and cereal, this is a healthy way to begin the day. Serve it on the rare morning that you wake up with the intention of changing your eating habits—at least until lunch. Experiment with your favorite fresh and frozen fruits.

CHIPS

- 5 flour tortillas
- 2 tablespoons butter, melted
- 1½ tablespoons cinnamon sugar

FRUIT SALSA

- 2 bananas, sliced
- 1 cup sliced strawberries
- 1 cup blueberries
- 1 teaspoon lime juice
- 1 teaspoon honey or sugar
- ½ cup yogurt, for topping the fruit salsa

Preheat the oven to 350°F.

Cut the tortillas into chip-size wedges. Pour the butter onto a plate or into a shallow bowl and toss the chips in melted butter; sprinkle with the cinnamon sugar.

Place on a baking sheet and bake for 10 minutes, or until golden brown.

Toss the fruit together in a bowl with the lime juice. Drizzle the honey over all and stir gently. Top with the yogurt. Serve with the chips for scooping. SERVES **2** TO **3**

granola

HOMEMADE GRANOLA is less than half the price of commercially packaged brands. You can make a big batch at once and give it as a hostess gift. It is a great recipe to have in your head. Once you get the swing of it, improvise with different fruits, nuts, seeds, and sweeteners. Serve with yogurt, ice cream, or fruit.

- 3½ cups quick-cooking oatmeal
- ¼ cup vegetable oil
- ¼ cup honey
- 1 tablespoon vanilla extract
- ½ cup raisins or other dried fruit, such as cranberries
- ½ cup chopped nuts
- ½ cup shredded coconut

Preheat the oven to 300°F.

In a large bowl, combine all ingredients, and then spread the mixture out on a baking sheet. Bake for 10 minutes.

When cool, break into small chunks and store in a jar or plastic container. MAKES **5** CUPS

slob smarts It takes 50,000 bees a year to produce 500 pounds of honey.

There is a vast difference between the savage and the civilised man, but it is never apparent to their wives until after breakfast.

—HELEN ROWLAND, A GUIDE TO MEN, 1922

go to bed mad, wake up with waffles

I COLLECT KITCHEN APPLIANCES, and I am especially fond of electric gadgets that cook on a tabletop. Waffles are favored over pancakes in our house, and I often mix up the batter the night before and keep it covered in the refrigerator overnight. Then I set the alarm ten minutes early, jig down to the kitchen, heat up the waffle iron, and make a stack. If I have extra, I wrap and freeze them and reheat the waffles in the toaster oven during the week.

For cornmeal waffles, replace 1/2 cup of the flour with cornmeal.

- **1 cup all-purpose flour**
- **1 teaspoon baking powder**
- **1/4 teaspoon baking soda**
- **1/4 teaspoon salt**
- **1 cup milk**
- **2 teaspoons fresh lemon juice**
- **2 tablespoons butter, melted**
- **1 egg, beaten**

Preheat a waffle iron and grease it.

In a large bowl, mix together the flour, baking powder, baking soda, and salt. Stir it around with a fork to give the impression of sifting without having to haul out the sifter.

Add the milk, lemon juice, and butter. Stir in the egg.

Bake on the waffle iron until steam stops coming out the sides.

SERVES **4**

slob smarts When making pancake and waffle batter, separate the eggs and whip the whites with a whisk until fluffy. Add the yolks to the milk, then fold in the whites for light, tender results.

french toast

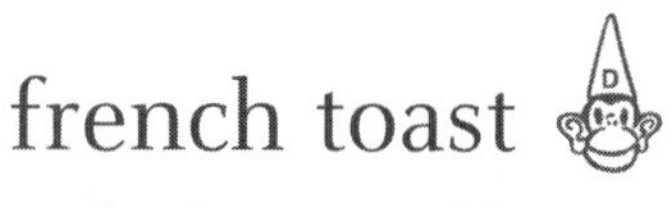

(cooked in a waffle iron)

PERFECT FOR MOTHER'S DAY, Father's Day, or any other guilt or appeasement day. It has the eggy richness of French toast and the crispy bits of fresh waffles.

- **3 eggs**
- **1 cup milk**
- **3 tablespoons sugar**
- **1 teaspoon vanilla extract**
- **¼ teaspoon cinnamon**
- **8 slices French bread or challah**

Preheat a waffle iron and grease it.

In a mixing bowl, whisk together the eggs, milk, sugar, vanilla, and cinnamon.

Soak the bread slices in the egg mixture, turning once.

Place a bread slice in the waffle iron, close, and cook until the bread is toasted and golden brown. Serve right away or put the finished slices in the oven at 200°F. while you make the rest. SERVES **4**

slob smarts To make one gallon of maple syrup, as much as fifty gallons of maple sap are required.

Only dull people are brilliant at breakfast

—OSCAR WILDE

chocolate crescents 

A RIP-OFF OF *PAIN AU CHOCOLAT.* It may sound a bit cheap and easy, but every time I make them, they are eaten right up.

- 1 tube of refrigerated crescent roll dough
- 2 ounces chopped semisweet chocolate or chocolate chips (about 1/3 cup)
- 1 egg
- 1/4 cup sugar

Unroll and separate the raw crescents. Sprinkle some chocolate bits in the center of each triangle, and roll up from the base to the point.

In a cup, beat the egg with 1 teaspoon of water to make an egg wash. Brush each roll with egg wash and sprinkle with sugar.

Bake according to package directions until golden. MAKES **8** CRESCENTS

slob smarts In the late 1600s, Vienna was under siege by the Turks. When Vienna was liberated in 1683, a baker made rolls in the shape of crescents to commemorate the victory over the Turks—thus the croissant was born.

My wife and I tried to breakfast together, but we had to stop or our marriage would have been wrecked.

—WINSTON CHURCHILL

faux nut doughnuts 

BY THE TIME you brew up a pot of coffee, you can have fresh doughnuts on the breakfast table; your guests will be knocked over by your ingenuity. These doughnuts have the delicacy of a pile driver.

The lanky Renée Zellwegger needed to gain thirty pounds in six weeks in order to reprise her role as the title character in *Bridget Jones, the Edge of Reason.* She consumed 4,700 calories a day, in part by eating doughnuts. "One doughnut doesn't do a thing," she said, "you've got to eat twenty a day for five weeks." This is a good recipe to have on hand next time Renée swings by your kitchen.

. . .

Separate a tube of refrigerated biscuit dough into individual biscuits. Punch a hole in the center of each biscuit by using the cap from a bottle of vegetable oil, making rings.

In a heavy saucepan, deep-fry the rings in 2 inches of hot vegetable oil for 2 minutes, flipping them once as they turn brown. Watch them closely; they cook quickly. Fry up the holes as well.

Drain them on paper towels and roll the doughnuts and holes in powdered, granulated, or cinnamon sugar.

If you drink enough coffee to get yourself motivated, ice them with some frosting; try 1 part powdered sugar and 1 part orange juice, whisk together, and pour over the doughnuts.

slob smarts Use a pot larger than your burner, especially when deep-frying. If the oil splatters it won't catch fire.

Hope is a good breakfast, but it is a bad supper.

—FRANCIS BACON

1-minute banana compote 

BANANAS CONTAIN THE CHEMICALS serotonin and epinephrine, which are believed to help prevent depression. This tastes so good, and is so easy to make, it's bound to make you happy.

I must make this three times a week. You can mix it with thick Greek yogurt or oatmeal or serve it on its own. My husband prefers it spooned on top of vanilla ice cream for a cheap facsimile of Bananas Foster.

- 1 banana, sliced
- 1 teaspoon butter
- 1 tablespoon brown sugar

In a microwaveable mug or bowl, combine the banana slices, butter, and brown sugar.

Microwave for 1 minute. Stir. SERVES **1**

All happiness depends on a leisurely breakfast.

—JOHN GUNTHER

breakfast spreads

PIE WAS OFTEN SERVED for breakfast in the nineteenth century, when it was considered a hearty and healthy way to begin a long day. Since most of us don't drive a team of oxen to work anymore, we tend to get by with coffee and toast. These spreads will make your toast a little more festive and take the sting out of cranky mornings. If you add some fruit and some protein, like an egg, cheese, or yogurt, you are well on your way to having a proper breakfast.

praline toast spread

In a small bowl, combine a knob of softened butter with some brown sugar and chopped pecans. If you have some unsweetened coconut flakes in your pantry, sprinkle it in to taste. Mash together with a fork to combine. Store covered in a small jar in the refrigerator.

cinnamon toast spread

Mix together some softened butter, a few shakes of cinnamon, and some brown or white sugar. Store in the refrigerator.

On its maiden voyage, the *Titanic* was stocked with 40,000 fresh eggs; 10,000 pounds of bacon, ham, and sausages; and 2,200 pounds of coffee.

lemon curd spread

I ADORE THE BRIGHT, shimmery rich taste of lemon curd on toast. This spread is a great filling for a cake or a prebaked pie shell.

1 ounce sweetened condensed milk
Juice and grated zest of 1 lemon
1 egg yolk

Stir the ingredients together in a bowl. Cover and refrigerate for 2 hours, or until thickened.

slob smarts Lemons contain more sucrose than strawberries.

chocolate toast

Mix 3 tablespoons sugar with 1/2 teaspoon cocoa powder. Sprinkle over 2 slices of toasted, buttered bread.

SLOB SMARTS

I picked up a list of common diner slang from my favorite neighborhood joint in the world, the BonBonnière. Marina, the waitress at this fine establishment, has fed me most mornings for nearly half my life, and I wrote quite a bit of this book on her counter.

- Adam 'n' Eve: two eggs
- Adam 'n' Eve on a raft, and wreck 'em: two scrambled eggs on toast
- Dry Whiskey Down: rye bread, toasted, no butter
- Burn the Brit: English muffin, toasted
- Lead Sinker: doughnut

appendixes

kitchen ammunition

In a French kitchen, the correct cooking tools are referred to as the *batterie de cuisine.* This is your arsenal of pots and pans and spoons and knives. In keeping with the warmongering reference, I present the following section, "Kitchen Ammunition." It isn't as daunting as a full *batterie de cuisine,* but it will give you a guideline to assist you when stocking your cupboards, cabinets, and larder.

stain removal

If you are a bit of a scrappy butterfingers, chances are so are your friends. Pull together a stain removal kit and keep it handy. It's not a party unless stuff gets broken, spilled, or knocked over. If you have a stain removal kit at the ready, then you can focus on the fun, not on the knucklehead who spilled red wine on your white carpet. The sooner you treat the stain the better the results will be.

COFFEE, TEA, WINE, JUICE: Cover with heaps of salt. The salt will draw the stains from the fibers. If a trace remains, use a stain remover to blot up the excess.

OIL (BUTTER, OIL, MAYONNAISE): Pretreat with stain remover or gently rub with liquid detergent. Wash in hot water with soapy detergent.

CANDLE WAX: Let harden, then scrape off the solid wax with a credit card. Treat with stain remover, then scrub by hand using hot water and liquid detergent.

LIPSTICK: Since it is a waxy, grease-based cosmetic, treat it with a prewash stain remover. If you have hairspray handy, spray some onto the stain. Let it sit for a few minutes, then wipe off the spray with a clean cloth. Wash in warm water with detergent.

INK: Hairspray works great as an ink remover.

guest removal

More stubborn than the toughest stain, the hardest thing to get off the sofa are your gasbag guests. Some techniques for removal are:

- Tell them the liquor has run out.
- Turn the lights up and the music off.
- Put on your pajamas and go to sleep.

We have a yodeling CD we refer to as guest repellent; it clears the room faster than a stink bomb. Find your own aural equivalent of Chinese water torture and keep it on hand for the night your party won't end.

clean as you cook

If you are a bit of a slob in the kitchen, the Vegas odds are in favor of your being less than fastidious in other rooms of the home, as well. The worst thing about cooking is that it creates the need for more cleaning—the two are unavoidably intertwined. Not being overly keen about either chore, I created an item that cleans while you cook: Dust Mop Slippers.

To remove the clammy fist of perfection pressing against your nose and to assist in your slovenly ways, I suggest you make yourself a pair. Purchase two dust mop replacement heads at the hardware store. Instead of inserting them on the business end of a dust mop, stick each foot into one of the attachment pockets, then lace the Velcro straps around your ankles, like ballet slippers. Once your feet are harnessed into the mop heads, glide around the house while you prepare dinner. By the time your meal is done, the floor will be sparkling clean. In fact, clean enough to eat off of. But don't.

I have dedicated quite a bit of effort to developing innovative ways to feed my family and clean our home. My husband says being married to me is like living with a combination of Benjamin Franklin and Lucy Ricardo. My lightning bolt of inspiration was to create a self-cleaning system for the kitchen and bathroom. I bought a bubble machine from a party supply store, rationalizing that the recipe for bubbles is soap and water.

I engaged the bubble machine and positioned a fan to blow the bubbles around the room and dry them once they popped. The results were a bit on the sticky side, but it is my fervent hope to perfect this system by the time the next edition of this book is printed.

In the interim, if you have a tiled room to clean, and for hygienic reasons can't wait for me to perfect my bubble machine method, I offer a simple alternative. I suggest that you squeeze some liquid gel dishwasher detergent onto the tile grout before you go to bed. When you take your morning shower, the dirt and detergent will rinse away. The room will be a lot cleaner than if you just let it sit there all by itself.

SLOB SMARTS
To make bubble solution, use three parts dish soap to one part water.

GARNISHES

A sprig of parsley or a sprinkle of paprika adds an earnest quality to your dishes and makes it look as though you tried.

Sprinkle dark stuff on light-colored food, and sprinkle light stuff on dark-colored food. It takes only a moment to add sliced lemon, a few grapes, or a few olives, but doing so creates a finishing touch that makes the food appealing.

Serve hot food on hot plates, cold food on chilled plates, and beer in frosty mugs.

pantry staples

If you stock your larder and pantry with staple ingredients you'll have a lot fewer excuses for avoiding cooking. Here is a guide to get you going in the right direction.

Baking powder
Baking soda
Basil, dried
Bay leaves
Beans, canned, or dried if you don't mind the soaking and cooking step. Keep chickpeas, white beans, and black beans on hand.
Bottled spaghetti sauce
Butter (sticks, not whipped, and unsalted is best)
Canned tomatoes, whole and crushed
Chicken stock or stock base
Cinnamon
Cloves, ground and whole
Cornstarch
Corn syrup
Flour, all-purpose (extra credit: bread flour, cake flour)
Garlic, fresh
Ginger, fresh and ground
Honey
Hot sauce (Tabasco and other brands)
Mayonnaise
Nutmeg
Olive oil
Onions
Oregano, dried
Paprika
Pasta: at least one long shape and one chunky one like penne or bowties
Peppercorns and a grinder
Rice
Salt
Soy sauce
Sugar: granulated, brown, and powdered
Tomato paste
Tuna (get oil-packed for best flavor)
Vanilla extract (considered an aphrodisiac, too!)
Vegetable oil, such as canola
Yeast

kitchen equipment

You don't need an arsenal of expensive kitchen equipment to cook the pants off of almost anyone. My cookware is a mismatched collection of castoffs and thrift-shop bargains. Here is a list of basic tools; if you don't have exactly what you need for a given recipe, use your head and improvise.

Baking dishes: lasagna-size and a 2-quart casserole are useful shapes
Baking sheets
Blender and immersion stick blender
Cake tins: 9-inch round and square
Can opener
Cast-iron skillet
Colander
Cutting board
Frying pans with lids: 10- and 12-inch
Grater
Knives: one good chef's knife with a 9-inch blade and a paring knife
Measuring cups for dry and liquid ingredients
Measuring spoons
Mixing plus serving bowls
Mixing plus serving spoons
Pasta pot
Pie plate
Roasting pan (the heavier the better)
Saucepan with lid
Spatula
Stockpot

equivalents

1 pound butter =	4 sticks
½ cup butter =	1 stick or ¼ pound
1 ounce =	2 tablespoons
1 pound brown sugar =	2¼ cups well packed
1 pound granulated sugar =	2 cups
1 pound powdered sugar =	3½ cups, sifted
1 pound white flour =	4 cups
1 pound whole wheat flour =	4½ cups
3 cups cooked rice =	1 cup uncooked
2 cups cooked pasta =	1 cup uncooked or 4 ounces
1 cup bread crumbs =	2 slices of standard sandwich bread
1 cup cracker crumbs =	12 graham crackers, 20 saltines, 24 vanilla wafers
2 cups grated cheese =	½ pound
1 cup chopped nuts =	¼ pound
1 cup chopped celery =	2 medium stalks
1 cup chopped onion =	2 medium onions
3 tablespoons lemon juice =	1 lemon
1 teaspoon grated lemon zest =	1 lemon
8 tablespoons orange juice =	1 orange
2 teaspoons grated orange zest =	1 orange

a glossary of cooking terms

BAKE. To cook with dry heat in an oven.

BASTE. To keep food moist during cooking by pouring a liquid over it; you can use meat drippings, melted fat, or any liquid.

BEAT. To make a mixture creamy, smooth, or filled with air by whipping it in a brisk motion.

BLEND. To stir two or more ingredients together until they are smooth and uniform throughout.

BOIL. To cook in a liquid at a temperature greater than 212°F. When boiling a liquid, you will see bubbles forming rapidly, rising continually and breaking when they reach the surface of the liquid.

BRAISE. To cook in a covered pan on top of the stove or in the oven, generally in a liquid.

BREAD. To coat a raw food with bread crumbs; the bread crumbs are often mixed with beaten egg, or the food is first dipped in the beaten egg and then coated with bread crumbs.

BROIL. To cook a food by placing it on a rack that is placed directly under the source of heat or directly over an open fire. To pan-broil is to cook the food in a heavy pan on top of the stove; the pan is usually ungreased, and any grease from the food is poured off as it accumulates so the food won't start to fry.

CHOP. To cut food in pieces about the size of small peas.

COOL. To remove a food from the source of heat and let it stand at room temperature until it reaches room temperature; food should not be put in the refrigerator to bring the temperature down more quickly.

CREAM (VERB). To mix one or more foods together until they are creamy and soft.

CUT IN. To use a knife or pastry blender to add shortening to dry ingredients; the shortening is actually cut into tiny pieces during the blending process.

FRY. To cook in a bath of hot fat.

GRILL. To roast over direct heat.

SAUTÉ. To cook in a small amount of fat.
SIMMER. To cook in water below 212°F. (boiling temperature).
STEAM. To cook food over the hot steam generated by a small amount of boiling water.
STEW. To simmer food in a small amount of liquid for a long period of time.

produce notes

What to look for, how to know what's ripe, and how to store it.

APPLES should have a rich, deep, uniform color; avoid bruised, soft, or blemished fruit. Hold at room temperature for 1 to 3 weeks; when cut, dip in lemon juice, cover in plastic wrap, and refrigerate to prevent the flesh from turning brown.

APRICOTS should have a deep color and a rosy blush and should be firm; avoid bruised, soft, or shriveled fruit. Store covered or uncovered in the refrigerator.

ARTICHOKES should be small with tightly closed leaves of uniform color; avoid those that are discolored or that have spreading leaves, and watch for insect infestation. Store uncovered in the refrigerator for 1 to 2 days.

ASPARAGUS should be tender with firm stalks and compact tips and should be 6 to 8 inches in length; avoid stalks that are whitish or that are too large or long. Store upright and covered in the refrigerator; use within 1 to 3 days to avoid toughening.

AVOCADOS should be dark, with either smooth or pebbled skin; they should yield to gentle pressure when ripe, and they will ripen during storage. Avoid fruit that is too dark and soft. Store covered or uncovered in the refrigerator. To ripen, store at room temperature. If cut, keep the pit in the fruit to preserve freshness, wrap in plastic, and refrigerate.

BANANAS should be firm and uniform in color. They will ripen during storage; avoid fruit that is soft, bruised, or spotted. Store at room temperature. If too ripe, unpeel and freeze.

BEETS should be small (3 inches in diameter maximum), with uniform deep red color. Store at room temperature; remove tops before storing.

BERRIES should be medium-size, uniform in color, firm, and plump; avoid berries that have started to "juice" or that have mold on them. Store unwashed, spread out in the refrigerator, covered; check frequently for mold.

BROCCOLI should be tight, close buds of uniform green color; avoid broccoli with yellow flowers or yellow buds or with smudgy spots. Store covered in the refrigerator.

BRUSSELS SPROUTS should be firm and deep green, with tight heads; avoid those that have started to wilt. Store covered in the refrigerator.

CANTALOUPE should have webbed skin with yellowish coloring underneath and a smoothly rounded depression at each end; the stem end should yield to slight pressure. It should have fragrant aroma. Avoid fruit that is sunken or that has a callused scar on the end. Cantaloupe ripens during storage; store at room temperature to ripen and in the refrigerator after it ripens; once cut, store tightly covered in the refrigerator.

CARROTS should have uniform bright orange color; store in the refrigerator.

CAULIFLOWER should have tight flower clusters, a firm head, and well-formed white flowers; avoid those with smudgy or dirty spots (which indicate insect infestation). Store covered in the refrigerator.

CELERY should be light, pale green; avoid celery that is too dark. Store in the refrigerator.

CORN should have blunt ends and darkened, dry silk. When a kernel is pierced with a fingernail, juice should spurt out. Avoid corn that has dried-out kernels, and watch for worms. Corn stays fresh longer if it is not husked; store in the refrigerator either covered (husked) or uncovered (in husks).

CUCUMBERS should be medium to dark green, long and slender, and firm; avoid cucumbers that are yellowed or soft with wrinkled skin. Store whole covered in the refrigerator.

EGGPLANTS should have a glossy shine and a deep purple color, and should be firm; avoid fruit that lacks glossy shine or that has green spots. Store whole and covered in the refrigerator.

GRAPEFRUIT should be heavy for its size, with smooth, thin skin; avoid fruit that is light for its size, has puffy skin, or has sunken, withered, or soft areas. Store either at room temperature or in the refrigerator; when cut, store tightly covered in the refrigerator.

GREEN PEPPERS should be firm, thick-walled, and deep green; avoid peppers that are wrinkled or soft or have uneven color. Store covered in the refrigerator.

HONEYDEW MELONS should be large (5 to 7 pounds), firm, and pale yellow or creamy white; avoid soft, small, or greenish fruit. Store at room temperature until cut, and then store tightly covered in the refrigerator.

LEMONS should be heavy for their size and should be deep yellow with uniform color and smooth, thin skins; avoid fruit with a greenish tinge or thick skins. Store at room temperature; lemons will yield more juice if warmed in a microwave oven for 20 seconds or in hot water for 15 minutes before juicing. Store cut lemons covered in the refrigerator.

LETTUCE should be heavy for its size, with a firm head and deep green leaves. Scratch the core and sniff; avoid those with a bitter smell, and avoid soggy or wilted heads. Store in a paper bag in the refrigerator (do not store in a plastic bag).

LIMES should be heavy for their size and uniform dark green in color; avoid those with pale color or those that are soft and wrinkled. Store at room temperature; store cut limes tightly covered in the refrigerator.

MUSHROOMS should be light in color, tightly closed around the stem, and well rounded; avoid mushrooms that are spotted, discolored, woody, or showing signs of decay. Store covered in the refrigerator.

ONIONS should be full, firm, and slightly flat with brown and shriveled tops; avoid those with wet necks or signs of mold. Store at room temperature.

ORANGES should be heavy for their size and should have smooth, thin skins; they may be deep orange or tinged with green, and they should be firm, but yield to pressure. Avoid oranges with sunken, withered, or discolored areas and oranges that are light for their size or have thick, puffy skin. Store at room temperature or in the refrigerator; store cut oranges covered in the refrigerator.

PEACHES should be firm with deep uniform color with a rosy blush; avoid those with a green tint or those with soft, brown, or bruised areas. Store covered or uncovered in the refrigerator.

PEARS should be slightly underripe, just turning yellow; firm; and slightly soft at the stem end. They ripen during storage. Avoid discolored, spotted, or bruised fruit. Store covered in the refrigerator when cut.

PINEAPPLES should have a small, tight crown, a sweet fragrance, and bulging eyes. The center leaves should come out easily when tugged gently, and it should make a dull, solid sound when thumped. Avoid those that are greenish, those whose stems don't pull out, or those with a fermented odor. Store at room temperature or in the refrigerator; when cut, store covered in the refrigerator.

POTATOES should be firm with a netlike texture on the skin, and should have shallow eyes and even color; avoid those with rot (unpleasant odor), green color (which indicates poison), or sprouted eyes (sprouts are poisonous). Store in a dark, cool, well-ventilated place away from light; do not store whole potatoes in the refrigerator. Cover cut potatoes with water and a few drops of vinegar, and store in the refrigerator for up to three days.

SWEET POTATOES should be small and firm and should be uniform rose to bronze in color; avoid those that are soft, shriveled, or blackened. Store at room temperature.

TOMATOES should be firm, but should yield to pressure. They should be heavy for their size and should have a deep uniform red color. Tomatoes ripen during storage; avoid those that are mushy, light for their size, or extremely hard. Store at room temperature. Also, cut a ripe tomato and rub it in your face and hands for a beauty treatment.

WATERMELONS should be rounded with filled-out ends, a smooth surface, and a creamy color on the underside; when scraped with a fingernail, the skin should yield thin green shavings. Avoid those with a shiny surface or creamy color on more than half their surfaces. Store in the refrigerator or at room temperature; store tightly covered in the refrigerator if cut.

ZUCCHINI should be shiny green. Store at room temperature. The enormous ones are tough, so save them for a curiosity and eat the small and medium-size ones.

hello gorgeous: beauty treatments to cook up at home

This section is a rich dietary source of beauty recipes.

You work hard cooking for everyone else, so please take the time to be good to yourself and try out one of these beauty recipes. As my dad said, "If you don't take care of your body, where are you going to live?" And who deserves it more than you? Make sure you're on your own checklist. It's never too late to get better looking or smarter, so get cracking. And remember, the only true cosmetic for beauty is happiness.

BUBBLE BATH

Pour 2 cups of vegetable oil, 3 tablespoons of mild baby shampoo, and a few drops of essential oil in a blender and hit the high-speed button for 10 seconds. Remember this the next time you pass the cosmetics counter and some knucklehead is charging $60 for a thimbleful of lime basil bath foam.

CITRUS PEEL BATH

Add 1 handful of orange, tangerine, lemon, lime, or grapefruit zest and 1 teaspoon vegetable oil to running bathwater.

HONEY BATH

Add 1/4 cup honey to warm bathing water. Honey has moisturizing properties and a great scent.

MINT BATH

Place 1 cup fresh mint leaves or 1/4 cup dried mint leaves in old pantyhose and dunk it in the tub. It wakes your tired ass right up.

EXFOLIATING STRAWBERRY FACE MASK

Crush a handful of strawberries and mix with 1 teaspoon honey. Apply to your face and leave on for 15 minutes.

FIRMING FACE MASK

Mix 1 tablespoon honey, 1 egg white, and 1/2 teaspoon vegetable oil. Smooth over your face. Leave on for 10 minutes and rinse.

HONEY AND LEMON CLEANSING FACE MASK

Combine the juice of 1/2 lemon, 1 1/2 teaspoons honey, 4 tablespoons plain yogurt, and 1 whipped egg white and apply to your face. Leave on for 15 minutes. Gently wipe off with a damp washcloth.

LEMON BLEMISH TREATMENT

Combine a pinch of cornmeal, a few drops of water, and a squirt of lemon juice to make a paste. Moisten a cotton swab with treatment and apply to blemishes.

BANANA HAIR CONDITIONING PACK

Mix 1 mashed banana with 1/4 cup honey. Massage into clean, damp hair. Wrap with a plastic cap or shower cap and cover with a towel to insulate your body heat. Rinse, then shampoo as usual.

HONEY HAIR SHINE

Stir 1 teaspoon honey into 4 cups warm water. After shampooing, pour the mixture through your hair. This is great for thick, coarse, frizzy hair like mine.

ROUGH SKIN TREATMENT

Combine 1 teaspoon honey, 1 teaspoon vegetable oil, and 1/4 teaspoon lemon juice. Rub onto elbows, knees, and ankles.

LAVENDER SOAP BALL

Using a cheese grater, grate 2 bars mild castile or vegetable-based soap into a bowl. Add lavender blossoms, 5 drops lavender essential oil, and enough water to make a stiff paste. Shape into balls. Let dry 2 days.

Every kitchen should be equipped with a dishwasher, preferably a neck-snappingly handsome fella wearing only an apron.

—LYNN FISCHER

I make no secret of the fact that I would rather lie on a sofa than sweep underneath it. But you have to be efficient if you're going to be lazy.

—SHIRLEY CONRAN

index

conversion chart

American cooks use standard containers, the 8-ounce cup and a tablespoon that takes exactly 16 level fillings to fill that cup level. Measuring by cup makes it very difficult to give weight equivalents, as a cup of densely packed butter will weigh considerably more than a cup of flour. The easiest way therefore to deal with cup measurements in recipes is to take the amount by volume rather than by weight. Thus the equation reads:

1 cup = 240 ml = 8 fl. oz. 1/2 cup = 120 ml = 4 fl. oz.

It is possible to buy a set of American cup measures in major stores around the world.

In the States, butter is often measured in sticks. One stick is the equivalent of 8 tablespoons. One tablespoon of butter is therefore the equivalent to 1/2 ounce/15 grams.

LIQUID MEASURES

FLUID OUNCES	U.S.	IMPERIAL	MILLILITERS
	1 teaspoon	1 teaspoon	5
1/4	2 teaspoons	1 dessertspoon	10
1/2	1 tablespoon	1 tablespoon	14
1	2 tablespoons	2 tablespoons	28
2	1/4 cup	4 tablespoons	56
4	1/2 cup		120
5		1/4 pint or 1 gill	140
6	3/4 cup		170
8	1 cup		240
9			250, 1/4 liter
10	1 1/4 cups	1/2 pint	280
12	1 1/2 cups		340
15		3/4 pint	420
16	2 cups		450
18	2 1/4 cups		500, 1/2 liter
20	2 1/2 cups	1 pint	560
24	3 cups		675
25		1 1/4 pints	700
27	3 1/2 cups		750
30	3 3/4 cups	1 1/2 pints	840
32	4 cups or 1 quart		900
35		1 3/4 pints	980
36	4 1/2 cups		1000, 1 liter
40	5 cups	2 pints or 1 quart	1120

SOLID MEASURES

U.S. and Imperial		Metric Measures	
OUNCES	POUNDS	GRAMS	KILOS
1		28	
2		56	
3 1/2		100	
4	1/4	112	
5		140	
6		168	
8	1/2	225	
9		250	1/4
12	3/4	340	
16	1	450	
18		500	1/2
20	1 1/4	560	
24	1 1/2	675	
27		750	3/4
28	1 3/4	780	
32	2	900	
36	2 1/4	1000	1
40	2 1/2	1100	
48	3	1350	
54		1500	1 1/2

OVEN TEMPERATURE EQUIVALENTS

FAHRENHEIT	CELSIUS	GAS MARK	DESCRIPTION
225	110	1/4	Cool
250	130	1/2	
275	140	1	Very Slow
300	150	2	
325	170	3	Slow
350	180	4	Moderate
375	190	5	
400	200	6	Moderately Hot
425	220	7	Fairly Hot
450	230	8	Hot
475	240	9	Very Hot
500	250	10	Extremely Hot

Any broiling recipes can be used with the grill of the oven, but beware of high-temperature grills.

EQUIVALENTS FOR INGREDIENTS

all-purpose flour—plain flour
baking sheet—oven tray
buttermilk—ordinary milk
cheesecloth—muslin
coarse salt—kitchen salt
cornstarch—cornflour
eggplant—aubergine
granulated sugar—caster sugar
half and half—12% fat milk
heavy cream—double cream
light cream—single cream
parchment paper—greaseproof paper
plastic wrap—cling film
scallion—spring onion
shortening—white fat
unbleached flour—strong, white flour
zest—rind
zucchini—courgettes or marrow